AMERICAN MAFIA: CHICAGO

AMERICAN MAFIA: CHICAGO

TRUE STORIES OF FAMILIES WHO MADE WINDY CITY HISTORY

WILLIAM GRIFFITH

GUILFORD, CONNECTICUT

Distributed by NATIONAL BOOK NETWORK

Library of Congress Cataloging-in-Publication Data

Griffith, William.
 American mafia : Chicago : true stories of families who made Windy
City history / William Griffith. — First Edition.
    pages cm
 Includes bibliographical references.
 ISBN 978-0-7627-7844-7
1. Mafia—Illinois—Chicago—History. 2. Organized
crime—Illinois—Chicago—History. 3.
Criminals—Illinois—Chicago—Biography. I. Title.
 HV6452.I32G75 2013
 364.10609773'11—dc23

                                2013015005

Printed in the United States of America

CONTENTS

INTRODUCTION

Some time ago I sat in a coffee shop with a neighbor in Chicago and he pointed at an old man walking down the street.

"See that guy?" he asked. "He's in the mob."

"Sure he is," I said. Some people around here think every old guy who walks his dog down the snowy streets while smoking a cigar is a former hit man.

"I had dinner with some friends at the Italian American social club a few years ago," he solemnly told me. "And the guy I was eating with pointed at that guy and said, 'You see him? He can look at a doorknob, just *look* at it, and make a key for it, and it'll work. It only takes him one try. See the guy next to him? It takes him two tries, but he can do it too.' They learned to do it in prison. They're Mafia."

This kind of conversation comes up a lot in Chicago—everyone, it seems, had a grandfather who was a jewel thief for the Grand Avenue crew, or who owned a little tailor shop that made suits for Al Capone. Not *all* of them are lying or mistaken, either. I always thought it was just ugly neighborhood gossip that the people in the Italian American social club—a group of old men who would sit on lawn chairs outside the building on the corner, laughing and shouting at one another—had mob ties, but I later found out that when a famous mobster, like Joey "The Clown" Lombardo, went missing, that club was one of the first places the feds looked. It was mostly just bookies in there, but the "big" guys liked it there too.

Chicago, 1915 NATIONAL ARCHIVES

By all accounts, the mob in the city is relatively quiet these days—even the most notorious hangouts and dens seldom contain anyone more sinister than a bookie or two. But stories of organized crime continue to haunt the city today; a historian can scarcely walk through a neighborhood without gruesome crime scenes flashing before his eyes.

Just walk down Grand Avenue near Racine—Lombardo had a day job in a masonry shop on the block for years.

That little Mexican restaurant was once a funeral home; "Samoots" Amatuna's funeral was held there.

That exterminator's shop used to be the grocery store where Terrible Tony Genna was gunned down.

That candy store was once a sandwich shop where Richard Cain, the double agent Boss Sam Giancana supposedly said was the man who killed John F. Kennedy, was himself shot down by masked gunmen in 1973.

Down the road, Halsted and Grand is the intersection where in 1929 a gangster was kicked out of a car after having been "taken for a ride." He was on fire when they threw him from the vehicle—they'd shot him, soaked his clothes in alcohol, and set him ablaze in the car before kicking his not-yet-dead remains into the road.

Everyone knows Chicago has a long history of mob stories, but how many of the people driving across the intersection today know *that* story now?

Most of the stories are forgotten now, buried among all the rumors and fictions created by pulps and gossip, but the city's true history of organized crime haunts it still. Go across the sea and tell someone you're from Chicago, and likely as not his or her response will be "Al Capone! Bang bang bang!" It may even be that Chicago can take credit for inventing the popular image of gangsters; Ben Hecht, a Chicago reporter who also wrote screenplays for a handful of notable gangster movies, supposedly claimed that he didn't really know how gangsters talked—he had just made up the dialogue in his scripts, and then the gangsters who went to his movies started to copy them. There's no reason to think this is exactly true. Hecht was never one to let facts get in the way of a good story, and some early accounts of gangster talk seem to indicate that plenty of them talked like they were in an Edward

Why they call it "bootleg." The fact that the woman posed for photographers showing how she hid her liquor shows how openly the law was flouted. LIBRARY OF CONGRESS

"Real beer" captured by authorities en route to Chicago from a suburban brewery that was supposed to be brewing "near beer." LIBRARY OF CONGRESS

G. Robinson movie long before "talkies" came out (in 1920 Nicholas "The Choir Singer" Vianna was quoted describing himself as "a real tough kid, right? Afraid of nuttin', see?"), but it's certain that the "Chicago" concept of gangsters fixed the world's impression of organized crime in the early twentieth century. Even in the 1920s, the gangsters and the reporters and writers formed a sort of symbiotic circle where each fed off the other.

Telling the whole story of Chicago gangland, with all its ever-twisting allegiances and tangled webs, would be impossible in one book. Rather than trying to create a complete guide, in *American Mafia: Chicago* I'll tell a few of the most fascinating stories from the early days, when loosely organized, incredibly secretive gangs terrorized neighborhoods with names like Little Hell through the mob's headiest years, when Al Capone and his men pretty well controlled the city.

I'd hate to call those Roaring Twenties years the "glory days." They were ugly times. People were killed—and not just mobsters, but unsuspecting people who paid seventy-five cents for "booze" that turned out to be juice mixed with embalming fluid, which is about as safe to drink as a glass of drain cleaner. Sometimes innocent civilians would get caught in the crossfire of a gangland drive-by. The lawlessness of the city paved the way for complete buffoons to be elected mayor.

But for better or worse, these are the stories that created the legend of Chicago, the legend that continues to grow around the world and down the cracked sidewalks of Grand Avenue, Taylor Street, and so many other places where the footprints are still on the ground.

Most of the buildings are gone now.

But the stories are still there, if you know where to look.

William Griffith
2013

Traffic in Chicago, 1917 NATIONAL ARCHIVES

CHAPTER ONE

Little Hell and the Black Hand

At the beginning of the twentieth century, Chicago was riddled with unsavory districts. Maps published in newspapers and police memoirs show "Shantytown" on the Lake Shore, where the Magnificent Mile is today, and "Satan's Mile" on South State Street in the now-respectable South Loop, which veered off into even nastier sub-neighborhoods with names like Hell's Half Acre, Coon's Hollow, Little Cheyenne (Cheyenne was known as one of the roughest of the old railroad towns), and Dead Man's Alley. Police traveled to these places in pairs when they went into them at all. Crimes were frequently unreported simply because no one wanted to admit to having *been* in the neighborhoods in the first place, since just being there strongly implied that you were frequenting whorehouses.

But perhaps the most lurid name was given to a residential neighborhood on the lower North Side—a broad patch just west of Halsted and just below Division Street that the papers called Little Hell.

Little Hell

At the intersection of Grand, Milwaukee, and Halsted was Little Sicily—a notoriously rough place decades before a gangster was shoved out of a moving car while burning alive there. But even the stories of Little Sicily paled in comparison to Little Hell, another Sicilian enclave a short hike away. Originally the eastern outcropping of a tough Irish neighborhood known as "Kilgubbin," Little Hell was in a class by itself.

The gateway intersection to the notorious region, which stood at Halsted Street and Chicago Avenue, was once claimed by the *Tribune* to be the dirtiest intersection in the world. A girl crossing the road in a pure white confirmation gown, it was said, "would resemble an alderman who had had an all night session with a city coal contract," while "a cherub flitting about this corner would have to spend the remainder of his days associating with the English sparrows that infest the district."

Given the fact that these claims were made in 1907, it's almost remarkable that the reporter didn't make a crack about a white person crossing the street and being mistaken for a player in a minstrel show. Racial and ethnic stereotypes that seem abhorrent to us today were tossed off very casually in the early twentieth century, and few people complained about them, at least out loud. A few decades before, when the *Chicago Times* (a paper that practically rejoiced in racism) invented the story about Mrs. O'Leary starting the Great Chicago Fire, papers had cheerfully spoken of Mrs. O'Leary's "typical Irish know-nothingness."

When it came to Italians and Sicilians, papers (and even progressive-minded reformers) spoke of one trait above all others: secrecy. Even in 1931, IRS documents relating to the Al Capone investigation would speak of his "native Italian secretiveness." Coming in at a close second was a penchant for revenge.

But this wasn't *all* just an ugly stereotype. The concept of *omertà,* the ancient code of personal honor that mostly survived as a "code of silence," had grown out of life in Italy and Sicily, which had long been governed by ineffective state governments and foreign powers. In the old country, people who wanted justice were usually left to their own devices. Distrust of authority ran deep and followed immigrants into their new country—to some, going to the police for help was considered an act of cowardice.

This code of honor ran deep and evolved. In Sicily it was the custom that if a man's girlfriend was unfaithful, he was entitled to scratch her cheek with the edge of a coin. Jane Addams of Hull House wrote that in America, the custom evolved into scratches with a knife.

Compounding this was the fact that the local authorities in Chicago in the 1910s weren't much more useful than the weak authorities in the old country had been. And they were almost never of any use in combating the street gangs that came to terrorize Little Hell in the early twentieth century. Speaking out against the gangs was dangerous. To many, the only way to deal with criminals was to fight back personally.

At the time when Little Hell was emerging as a neighborhood, Americans were first seeing the term *mafia* in newspapers. Exactly where the word came from is the subject of much debate. Among the more common theories is that it came from an old Italian acronym for *Morte Alla Francia Italia Anela* ("death to the French is Italy's cry"), which emerged during riots in 1282 after a French officer killed a Sicilian woman, but this is really little more than wild speculation. Like much to do with the Mafia, its true origin is something of a mystery.

The section of Little Hell known as Death Corner averaged nearly a murder per week in the 1910s. CHICAGO HISTORY MUSEUM

In those early twentieth-century days, it was still plausible to deny that the Mafia was an actual group at all. In 1914 the *Tribune* explained, "The 'mafia' is not in any real sense a secret society. It is rather a code of conduct, a system of life into which many Sicilians are born and into which they have been trained for more than a thousand years."

Maybe it really *wasn't* a secret society at the time, at least not in Chicago, but that "code of conduct" would soon become associated with bands of criminals that were rapidly getting more organized—especially in Little Hell. The neighborhood was only about thirty years old by the time the word *mafia* first starting coming up in the press, but it was already looking old and shabby by then. The tumbledown shacks and frame houses hadn't looked *that* good when they were first built in the 1870s, after the Great Chicago fire destroyed the shacks that had been there before, but by the early 1900s they were looking particularly worse for wear. The paint was universally faded and chipped on the buildings that had ever been painted at all. The streets were narrow, and few streetlights had ever been added. Sanitation was almost unheard of, and dust blew in from the coal yards and train lines constantly, coating the buildings in a layer of grime. Nearly every reporter who ventured into the place noted the crowds milling about outside of the saloons at all hours.

"By day," wrote one, "one wanders through the district and these loungers appear mild and innocent-looking. By night they seem to take on the appearance of their real nature. They become bolder as it becomes dark. Their sharp little eyes peer insolently into the face of the pass-erby. It is obvious that strangers are not wanted over here and that everyone is under suspicion."

Most reporters still took pains to point out that many of these immigrants were honest, hardworking, and upright. The children there—and there were a lot of children—seemed happy as they ran through the streets, freely alternating between speaking English and Italian. Indeed, when a 1908 medical inspection of slums was made, Little Hell was found to be a bit ahead of the curve in terms of sanitation and nutrition. While babies elsewhere were found to be eating terrible diets (several were living on nothing but pasta or sour milk) and kept in dangerous conditions, mothers in Little Hell were said to be "alive to the dangers for their babies in the hot-weather waves. The milk is kept clean, the food is wholesome, and there is good ventilation. In fact, it would seem that Little Hell is being redeemed at last."

But in 1908, even if basic living conditions appeared to be improving, stories of crime were on the rise in the district, and stories about Little Hell for the next decade would be dominated by stories about the gangs that terrorized the area. These gangs were collectively known as the Black Hand.

The Black Hand

Whenever a person in one of the city's Italian enclaves came into a piece of property, he could almost be sure to get a "Black Hand letter" demanding a huge sum of money, often signed with a drawing of a skull and crossbones or a dagger. If the money was not paid, the people who sent the letter started their retaliation by bombing the property. If the money still wasn't paid, letters would come threatening the lives of the recipient's family. Any word to the police, of course, meant instant death.

No one ever seemed to be sure at the time whether the Black Hand was really just one gang or a bunch of smaller groups that simply operated under the same tactics of extortion. Most historians now agree that the Black Hand was a modus operandi, not one big gang. But Black Hand activities seemed to be widespread, to say the least. One newspaper estimated that one in four Italians in the city had paid tribute to the Black Hand at one point.

Black Hand crimes were famously hard for police to solve, and even when arrests were made, there were shockingly few convictions. At one point a group of Sicilian civil leaders organized a group called the White Hand to combat the criminals and met with some limited success, but the arrests made with their help usually ended with the suspects being freed. The group was organized in 1907 and seems to vanish from the record about five years later. The Black Hand was only just reaching the height of its fame by then.

Typical of the stories of Black Hand victims was that of Mrs. Antonina Locascio,* who lived on Cambridge Avenue, just below Division, in the heart of Little Hell, in 1915. Down the block and around the bend from her squat frame house was the intersection of Oak and Milton (now Oak and Cleveland), which papers had referred to as "Death Corner" for a decade—murders seemed to occur there every week.

Mrs. Locascio had been living for some years in the neighborhood with her husband and eight living children—not an unusually large family for the neighborhood. The family ran a little grocery store on Gault Court, and in 1914 they lived in a tenement at 940 North Milton—right at Death Corner—and her daughter Angelina had recently married a man named Joe Ingo.

One day they received a Black Hand letter demanding a payment of $1,000—a huge amount for a family in the slums, where most men couldn't hope to earn much more than that in two or three years of hard labor. Though friends told them to ignore the letter, one of the older children immediately boarded up the windows of their small apartment, and the family refrained from going out after dark. The "mafia," they were told, only shot at night. They were still safe by day, and eventually the whole affair would blow over.

Joe Ingo, young Angelina Locascio's husband, began to grow bolder and venture out more than the others. One night he came across a familiar face: Frank Jabbio,

* Mrs. Locascio's name is variously given as Antonina, Antoinina, and Angelina. I've gone with Antonina, the way her name is spelled on her death certificate. The last name varies in every report as well.

whose family had known the Locascios back in the old country. Jabbio had fled to New Orleans after the murder of a police officer there, only to flee Louisiana after a botched kidnapping case led to the hanging of his brother and the imprisonment of his sister. Now Jabbio had set up a life for himself in Chicago and was sometimes called the "King of the Black Handers." He wanted to chat with Joe Ingo, who apparently knew some dark secret about him.

Exactly what Joe knew about Jabbio that everyone else didn't is unknown—perhaps Joe thought he could use the information as leverage to have the Black Hand threats against his wife's family stopped. He arranged to meet with Jabbio at a saloon near the family's grocery store.

But the meeting was a short one. Jabbio came into the saloon with a sawed-off shotgun, fired at Joe before he could say a word, then immediately fled into the maze of back alleys and basements that connected every house in the neighborhood.

Joe stumbled bleeding into the street and fell to the ground. Angelina, having heard the gunshot, ran to his side. He lived just long enough to tell her that it was Jabbio who had fired the shot and that a man named Tony Morano had come in with him. He died in his young wife's arms.

Angelina, defying the unwritten code of the neighborhood, went to the police and told them her story. They promised to bring the killers to justice, but for one reason or another, nothing came of it. Nothing ever did in Little Hell.

Jabbio and Morano were taken in by the police but managed to convince authorities, at least for a time, that the real shooter had been Angelina's brother, Michael Locascio. Michael was briefly taken to jail, where he received daily threats from the Black Hand. Eventually

Federal building in Chicago after a bombing attempt during the Black Hand era, 1918. Hundreds of private business owners who didn't meet the Black Hand's demands shared a similar fate.
NATIONAL ARCHIVES

police abandoned the idea that he was the shooter and let him go, focusing their investigation back on Jabbio.

Michael was free of the authorities but not from the gangs, from whom he began to receive more letters:

"You talk too much. We will have to stop you with bombs."

A guard was set up around the Locascio house, but Mike continued to work to find out what secret Joe Ingo might have known about Jabbio. Eventually a man named "Prizzi" told Mike that Jabbio and his men had set fire to a Milwaukee Avenue pool room for the insurance money and that Ingo had known about it.

A week later Prizzi's body was found riddled with bullets, and the letters from the Black Hand became more and more threatening.

On December 1, Mrs. Locascio received the scariest letter yet:

> *It has come to our knowledge, old witch, that you could have paid us the money which we demanded and saved your son-in-law from death. Now he is in the cemetery and his corpse cries for vengeance! Vengeance! Vengeance! His soul has sent us for revenge, and now you must come forth with $1500, otherwise we will destroy all of you pretty soon. Look for friends and get it if you have not the money, otherwise we will use our terrible arms, and as you know we can never fail to kill you.*
>
> *LA MANO NERA (The Black Hand)*

Three days later a bomb exploded in the Locascio home. All the family members escaped, but one distraught son, twenty-four-year-old Giuseppe, later committed suicide by taking poison. He explained to his mother on his deathbed that he simply could not stand the abuse any longer. (The family had previously hoped that Giuseppe's marriage to a girl from the gang's family would put an end to the feud, but it was not to be.)

Even though the death certificate clearly lists Giuseppe's death as suicide by taking bichloride of mercury, the Black Hand took credit for the killing in another letter that arrived shortly thereafter to remind Mrs. Locascio that the money had still not been paid:

Old Witch: We are not at the end of the vengeance. You have been conscienceless and have made your own son and son-in-law be killed. But you have not yet paid. Now we give you three days' time, and if the money does not reach us by then the bomb and the carbine with the never-missing bullets will get you and your daughter and all your family. Beware, the vengeance is nearing!

Below the letter were drawings of three daggers.

The family scattered, fleeing all over Chicago. They didn't tell their new addresses to any friends or relatives, but everywhere they went they continued to receive the Black Hand letters. Eventually Mrs. Locascio decided it was time to face the problem head on and moved back to Little Hell, renting an apartment on North Cambridge Avenue. By now, Jabbio himself had been forced to flee Chicago, but the letters kept coming. The family traced them back to one Pietro Catalanetto, who was said to have taken over as "King of the Black Handers."

Mike Locascio arranged to meet with Catalanetto to pay the money, but the new "king" never made it to the meeting. He was on his way there when he was shot and killed near Division and Sedgewick, mere blocks from the Locascios' Cambridge Avenue apartment.

Mike had secretly arranged to tell the police about the meeting. But he decided against informing the police at the last minute, opting instead to take the vengeance he believed was his right and shoot Catalanetto down in front of the Criterion Theatre.

Mike fled after Catalanetto's murder, but the police, suspecting him of the killing, summoned Mrs. Locascio to the coroner's inquest to tell of her dealings with the gang.

"I will never leave that inquest alive," she said. "But I will go, and pay if I must."

On the morning of the inquest, she sat on the steps of her apartment with her husband and Angelina, who was still grieving the loss of her husband, and Angelina's young son, Frank.

At noon the scene in the neighborhood seemed calm. The *Tribune* described the scene in nostalgic terms: "Squat two story buildings, apparently crammed to bursting with dark-skinned men and women, and over-flowing with their dark-skinned children, were giving off odors of garlic from midday meals. Here and there the notes of an accordion floated from a window crowded with humanity. Children played tag in the open street and bickered with a fruit peddler."

But the calm was broken when two men approached the Locascios' stoop with revolvers drawn. The two calmly walked forth—later reports indicate that one of the men gave the "sign of death," pressing his bony thumbs to his forehead, then dragging a finger along his neck.

Mr. Locascio, Antonina's husband, noticed the sign right away. *"La Mano Nera!"* he shouted. "The Black Hand!" He grabbed little Frank and ran for the door as the men approached.

Antonina began to stand up to follow but never made it to her feet before the air was cut with the sounds of six gunshots. She dropped to her feet and tumbled to the ground dead, the basket of vegetables she was carrying spilling out onto the street.

The two men continued to march toward the door, firing a gun at it, but one of the bullets hit the lock on the door, causing it to jam and effectively keeping the two men out. One of them cursed, and the two men turned back, stopping only to kick Mrs. Locascio's lifeless body as her blood spilled over Cambridge Avenue. They tossed their pistols into a vacant yard and disappeared into the usual maze of alleyways.

Police expressed the opinion that, given the over-crowded nature of every building in the neighborhood, the two killers had probably slipped into a random house, taken off their coats, and sat down for a game of cards with the men who would inevitably have been seated around in the front room of the house, hiding in plain sight.

That night Mrs. Locascio's body lay beside Pietro Catalanetto's in a Division Street morgue, and word spread that Mrs. Locascio had been killed because she was going to violate *omertà*—the "law of silence." John and Phillip Catalanetto, Pietro's sons, were named by witnesses as the slayers and arrested, but after a dis-agreement among the jury at their trial, they were even-tually freed.

John was killed a year later on a streetcar, proba-bly by one of the Locascios. "I never saw such a look of hate on a man's face as on that of the Italian who shot John Catalanetto," said the conductor who was driv-ing the streetcar at the time. Police believed that John had known his killer and that Philip and his sister both knew perfectly well who it was—but they would not vio-late *omertà* and name him. The killer went free.

This was typical of a Black Hand story—at its heart the story was simply a family feud that had followed the two families to Chicago from the old country. But as the streets and the feud became deadlier, the "families" turned into gangs, and the original reason for the feud was probably long forgotten.

A victim of the Black Hand: Mrs. Locascio's death certificate
PUBLIC RECORD

The Mysterious Shotgun Man

Over the years, the Catalanetto and Locascio feuds dis
appeared in the dust of history, along with the neighborhood itself. When people decades later spoke of Little Hell
and the Black Hand, most of the stories began to revolve
around a largely mythical character known as "Shotgun
Man," who was sometimes said to have killed over one
hundred people at Death Corner, the intersection of Oak
and Milton.

Death Corner had certainly become a dangerous
place to be by the time of the Locascio feud—by some
estimates there was a murder there every week from
about 1905 through the end of the 1910s, when extortion

by mail became a federal offense and a federal government crackdown basically put an end to the practice (with some help from the rising class of better organized mobsters, who wanted the small-time Black Handers out of the way). Most of the hundreds of murders at the gruesome corner remained unsolved.

In many modern accounts of life in Little Hell, a mysterious "Shotgun Man" is estimated to have been responsible for at least a third of the killings at Death Corner. Stories of the Shotgun Man are not new; lurid diagrams of his method of working were published in the papers a century ago. In front of a grocery store on Oak Street a stairwell led into a basement entrance to the store and to a runway that connected to the other alleys and byways of Little Hell. At the bottom of this staircase, the Shotgun Man would stand at the ready, waiting for his victim to come around the corner of Milton onto Oak. As soon as the victim came into view, the Shotgun Man would fire off a load of buckshot, discard his weapon, and flee down the runway. This would all be done so quickly that men in the next building wouldn't even look up from their card game.

Certainly a lot of murders at Death Corner took place in just this way, and there *were* at least a few cases where a man matching that description was witnessed carrying out a shooting there. But blaming hundreds of them on one lone Shotgun Man is mostly a modern creation. In 1910 three or four murders happened all at once, and police did, in fact, say the suspect was a "shotgun man," but those three or four were all that could be traced to one man. Having one man be behind all the shootings would require the Black Hand to be one large organization, not a bunch of smaller ones.

Still, the idea that it *was* all one organization, with one man operating as the hit man, had a sort of romantic appeal that captured people's imaginations.

And throughout the city, "vice lords," safe crackers, and gang leaders were turning the myth into a reality. Soon the names of the leaders of gangs far more powerful than any Black Hand group would be known to every person in Chicago, and a few would be famous around the world in a way that a thug like Jabbio never could have imagined.

CHAPTER TWO

Il Diavolo and the Devil's Gang

The guards of the old prison that stood at the corner of Illinois and Dearborn were not easy men to frighten. They'd seen everyone do everything, and part of their job was attending executions that occasionally got a bit gruesome. Local laws required bodies to hang for twenty minutes to make sure they were dead, and sometimes it took them just about that long to die. In one case the rope broke, and the convict, one George Painter, ended up landing on his head. He was bleeding so much that they were fairly sure he was already dead, but the law required him to hang by the neck for the full twenty minutes. The bloody body was brought back up to the scaffold, a new noose was applied, and the man—by now possibly already a corpse—was slid down the trap door to dangle by his neck.

Other times hysterical men had to be tied to chairs to be hanged, and the chairs would spin obscenely at the end of the rope as the convict died.

Many convicts on death row made friends with the guards, and the prison officials sometimes led the condemned to the gallows with heavy hearts. Occasionally the guards would become so friendly with the condemned that they'd refuse to walk them to the scaffold at all—they just didn't have the heart to lead a friend to his death.

But no one wept to see gang lord Sam Cardinella[*] put to death in 1921. Cardinella scared the heck out of the guards. He would pace around in his cell like a venomous spider, glaring at them with empty eyes.

Cardinella had planned countless robberies—probably hundreds—and dozens of murders, but he seldom got his own hands dirty. His technique would largely set the template for the organized crime lords to come, with one critical difference: Most of his gangsters were teenagers. Some were little more than children.

An immigrant from Sicily, Cardinella lived with his family on South LaSalle in the notorious "levee" district below 12th Street. It would be there, not in Little Hell, that true organized crime began to blossom. Restaurant owner James Colosimo was part of the local government and actively worked to stamp out Black Hand operators who made his *own* scams, rackets and vice rings, harder to run. At 2222 South Wabash stood the Four Deuces nightclub, which was owned by Johnny "The Fox" Torrio. Under Colosimo's control at the time, Torrio had recently brought a young man named Alphonse Capone to Chicago to work in his organization.

Men like Colosimo and Torrio were already working to get the vice and gambling rings in the city organized, and in the 1920s these organized criminals would practically control the city. But in the late 1910s the smaller Cardinella gang was working right under their noses,

....
[*] Again, the spelling of Cardinella's name varies from document to document. Various records have him as Cardinelli, Cardanella, and Cardinale. Cardinella is perhaps the most common, so I've gone with that one.

enshrouded in such secrecy that no one realized that the holdups and killings they carried out in the neighborhood were even connected.

Reading about Cardinella and his crimes, one might think that he had read *Oliver Twist* and considered it a how-to manual. Cardinella had opened a pool hall on 22nd Street, where he brainwashed his underage customers into carrying out crimes on his orders. Some actually claimed he had supernatural powers over the boys to keep them under control (and some of the boys probably believed he did). Some described the group as almost a cult, a band of robbers engaging in highly ritualized murders. Some even compared them to Hindu Thugees, the murderous Indian sect whose ritualized crimes were becoming fodder for dime novels.

The amount of ritual involved in the Cardinella gang's crimes was probably exaggerated, but the brutality of the gang, and of their heartless leader, needs no embellishment.

Once they had wandered into the pool hall, Cardinella would intimidate and manipulate the neighborhood boys into following his orders. He turned the poolroom into what papers would describe as a "college of crime" where the "murder clique" learned their trade. After teaching them techniques for holdups and killings, Cardinella would send the boys out on burglaries, take most of the money for himself, and then, often as not, cheat them out of their own share with a pair of loaded dice.

But the jobs they pulled were done so carefully and skillfully that police had no idea that most of the burglaries going on in the neighborhood were connected. Italian women in the area are said to have suspected they were, though. No one knew who the leader of the gang was, but he was referred to in whispered tones as "Il Diavolo," Italian for "The Devil."

Had Cardinella hung on a few more years, he theoretically could have become one of the bootlegging kingpins and expanded his empire tremendously—he had the brains and the ruthlessness it took to get ahead, not to mention the required sense of secrecy. But it seems as though he kept his hands away from the other gangs. There are no reports of his having meetings with Johnny Torrio, Big Jim Colosimo, or Alderman "Bathhouse" John Coughlin—three men most neighborhood gang lords should have known very well if they didn't want trouble. Cardinella and has gang were secretive enough to stay off their radar, and his technique of sending kids out to commit crimes for him worked well for some time. Who would suspect that a group of kids was part of a larger network?

One of his recruits was a popular, clean-cut young man named Nicholas Viana. Viana had wandered into the pool hall on 22nd Street on his way to choir practice one afternoon; he had seen other boys his age in there, and it looked like a fun place to spend a few minutes.

A week after he first entered the pool hall, Viana committed his first murder.

In the poolroom, Cardinella gave the kids a long list of rules. He warned them never to trust a woman, not even their mothers. He warned them never to brag or boast, or "squawk." People who squawked were killed. And he insisted on loyalty. Getting out of the gang was probably impossible. Most likely, none of Cardinella's boys believed he could leave the gang without being killed—probably along with a few of his family members.

By the time the gang was broken up in 1920, they were likely responsible for hundreds of holdups and for at least twenty murders, a dozen of which were committed by Viana alone. Under Cardinella's influence,

Nicholas "The Choir Singer" Viana had become one of the most cold-blooded killers in the history of the city—before reaching the age of nineteen.

Police certainly seemed to have suspected a gang was at work, and may even have uncovered a bit of information on them, but trying to get more clues proved frustrating. In 1918 two police detectives were shot while trying to question members of the band (both recovered).

The police got their first clue as to Il Diavolo's identity after a man named Andrew Browman was murdered in his saloon at 447 West 22nd

One of few known images of Sam Cardinella, the man they called "Il Diavolo." PUB-LIC RECORD

Street, not far from the poolroom. Seven kids had wandered in shouting "Stick 'em up!" and shooting blindly into the saloon.

A witness noted the license plate number on their getaway car, and police traced it to a man named Santo Orlando. When Orlando was arrested, the police questioned him for a few days before letting him go, unable to connect him to the robbery itself. Naturally he vanished shortly after his release.

Cardinella told the boys he'd had to rush Orlando out of town disguised as a woman.

"It cost me money to get rid of him too," he told them. The look in his eyes must have told them that there would be consequences for this. He took out a knife and told them that since they'd been involved in the robbery that got Orlando caught, they'd have to pay him back the money he'd spent to get Orlando out of town. A carpenter nearby was thought to have some money hidden, and Cardinella gave them explicit instructions on how to get it.

"Here's a stiletto," he said as he handed a knife to one of the boys. "Take it and stick it in his stomach. He's quiet and doesn't like to talk. But if you twist the knife around, he'll talk fast enough. When he tells you where the money is, shove the knife clear in and kill him."

Some time later, Orlando's body was found in a canal, riddled with eighteen bullet holes.

Cardinella underestimated the boys' loyalty to their friend Santo Orlando. When they learned that Cardinella had had him killed, and may even have done the deed himself for once, they began to turn against him. When the headquarters was raided a short while later, several boys who were arrested began to tell what they knew.

Soon Cardinella was in custody, along with more than a dozen gang members, and the newspapers published breathless reports exposing him and his "murder clique." Police called the raid on the gang's headquarters "the most important crime roundup in the city's history" and hoped Cardinella could be connected to any number of the dozens of unsolved "Black Hand" cases in addition to the many holdups and murders he was thought to have ordered. Papers initially stated that the gang was responsible for five murders, but the tally rose quickly as the boys told more and more stories. Cardinella himself was charged with the murder of a saloonkeeper; Viana and two of the other boys had actually done the killing, but as leader of the gang, Cardinella was held to be responsible for it.

The chief physician of the county jail, Frank McNamara, would later call Sam Cardinella "a spinner of death—a human spider who wove a fabric of assassinations and lurked in the shadows while younger men, some of them hardly more than boys, carried out his fatal instructions." Each of the crimes, it was written, was "as baffling in itself as a single piece of a jigsaw puzzle."

The Gang Laid Low

Unlike most of the Black Hand cases, the trials of the Cardinella gang were swift and brutal. More than ten of the gang members were sentenced to hang—including Cardinella.

Meanwhile, the gang members still on the outside hadn't exactly gone straight. They still seemed to be governed to some extent by some form of *omertà*. In August, a few months after the convictions were handed down, Frank Gibbia, a suspect in the killing of Santo Orlando, was found full of bullet holes in a car on the southern outskirts of the city. The *Tribune* said that "the hand of the *Camorra* reached out again from gang land yesterday and robbed the gallows of another member of the Cardinella gang." Orlando and Gibbia had lived together at one point in Little Hell on North Milton Street, just a block and a half north of Death Corner.

About half of those sentenced to death were eventually executed. Among the first was Nicholas "The Choir Boy" Viana, who was hanged for his nineteenth birthday on a cold December morning.

"When I first entered Cardinella's poolroom," he said, "I was a boy in short trousers. Within a week I was a criminal. After I was arrested, Cardinella threatened to kill my mother and my three sisters if I gave the police any information."

The reticent boy in his cell must have seemed unrecognizable to the people who knew him in the poolroom. When Nick was only seventeen, he was known as one of the fiercest members of the gang, which was no small honor. He thought Cardinella appreciated him. Cardinella called him a "real guy," a true compliment in that world. But he soon learned that Cardinella didn't care about him in the least; he was just a tool to him, as expendable as a bit of twine that came on a package. He was just another kid who could be brainwashed into killing people for six bucks a hit.

It's difficult now to figure out what kind of guy Viana really was. Papers at the time were not shy about putting quotes in the mouths of prisoners, especially those who were young or who had funny accents. In some papers Viana was quoted talking like a movie gangster ("afraid o' nothin', see?"). In others his speeches sounded like monologues from a bad Horatio Alger book as he piously spoke of the mistakes that led to his downfall and his hopes that other boys would learn the dangers of idleness from his wretched example. It's possible that both portraits are accurate and that his early toughness gave way to a more reserved, cooperative young man as he got out from under Cardinella's thumb.

But even though giving more information might have saved his neck (there was a loud public outcry against hanging him, and a bit more cooperation on his part probably would have tipped the scales), there were some things he refused to tell. He had been told through the prison "grapevine" that if he gave up any information at all, his mother and sister would be murdered for sure. He was still afraid of Cardinella and didn't believe his old master would truly be hanged. "He'll beat this yet," he told reporters.

Nick arranged to be hanged on December 9, 1920—the day he turned nineteen. He said that he thought it would be amusing to be hanged for his birthday.

But it turned out that The Devil may not have been done messing with him yet.

Probably oblivious to the fact that Cardinella still had plans for him, on the eve of his execution, Viana railed against his old boss to any reporter who would listen. He stopped short of giving more information but made his feelings about his old boss perfectly clear. "He is responsible for what will happen tomorrow," said Viana. "And yet, last week he sent word to me asking to write a letter to people on the outside saying he was innocent. Imagine this! The man who is responsible for my downfall, my going into crime, asking such a thing of me. All I want is that Cardinella hang—that's what he deserves!"

Much was made of Viana's skills as a singer. As he was escorted from his cell to the "death cell," the comfortable library where condemned men often spent their last night, he sang out "Il Miserere" from *Il Trovatore*, to the delight of prisoners and guards. "Beat any show you ever saw," one of the guards later remembered. His mother visited the death cell, and at her request he sang Kipling's "Mother o' Mine" to her:

> *If I were hanged on the highest hill,*
> *Oh mother o' mine, mother o' mine*
> *I know whose love would follow me still*
> *Oh mother o' mine, mother o' mine*

He insisted on the gallows that he was dying for his mother and sisters—he could have given information that might have saved his neck but declined for fear of their safety. At least one paper reported that his last words were, "Good-bye, boys. Good-bye to all but Sam Cardinella. May his soul be damned!"

The Devil's Last Trick

After his hanging, Viana's body was taken down and given to his friends, who put it in a wire basket instead of a coffin and loaded it into an ambulance instead of a hearse. The prison officials shrugged their shoulders. This wasn't the usual way of doing things, but perhaps it was one of those Sicilian traditions the guards never fully understood.

As his own execution approached, Cardinella began to refuse to eat. He was mean and hostile to the guards and paced endlessly about in his cell. Remembering the scene years later, Dr. McNamara felt that there was "a sense of ill omen, of menace, of mysterious evil" in the air around the prison.

The night before the execution, Cardinella was visited in the death cell by his wife and six children, the youngest of whom were told that their father was going "on a journey."

The scene with Cardinella's family was an emotional one. Guards were disquieted to see "the devil" acting like a penitent family man. He was weeping openly now, not displaying a bit of the toughness he was known for. Sam spoke with them in the Sicilian dialect his gang had favored—and that no one in the prison could quite understand. But one word he repeated several times stuck out: "Viana."

No one could guess why, in his last moments with his family, he would be talking about Nicholas "The Choirboy" Viana, the kid he blamed for his impending execution.

That night Cardinella didn't sleep for a second in the prison library, the "death cell" where condemned men traditionally spent their last nights. Prisoners on their last nights generally chatted with the guards, smoked, drank coffee, and tried to find ways to distract their minds from the fatal morning ahead. But all Cardinella did was pace back and forth "like a nervous tiger in a zoo," as McNamara put it.

Even when offered the chance to order anything he wished from a nearby restaurant as his last meal, Cardinella refused to eat. As he was led to his doom, he was weak on his feet, barely able to stand. He had lost as much as forty pounds. As they took him to scaffold, he threw himself on the ground and refused to stand up. He wailed in anguish, kissed the feet of the police, and, by some accounts, lost control of his bodily functions (which was not particularly uncommon among the condemned). The disgusted guards had to tie him to a chair in order to hang him, as they'd done a few times before with others. The chair swung gruesomely about when it dropped from the scaffold, and Cardinella's neck was fractured.

Many papers—even a short Ernest Hemingway story—made light of Cardinella's breakdown. Here was the most fearsome, heartless killer in town, cowering in fear and unable to face his doom like a man! Where was his nerve now?

But Hemingway and the reporters had no idea what was truly going on.

After the hanging, the body was given to friends, who put it in a wire basket and brought it to an ambulance, just as they'd done with the remains of Nicholas Viana. A couple of people in nurse's uniforms were seen hanging around the jail.

This time the warden suspected something was amiss. He delayed the ambulance and Cardinella's remains in the jail yard for an hour while the other two men scheduled to die that day were hanged. He then ordered that the body be put in a funeral car to be taken to the morgue.

When the cops looked into the ambulance, they were shocked at what they saw: A woman in a nurse's outfit was rubbing Cardinella's lifeless wrists, cheeks, and neck. A doctor was holding a hypodermic needle, ready to inject something into the dead man's chest.

They were trying to bring the corpse of Sam Cardinella back to life.

It turned out that Cardinella's refusal to eat, his pacing, and his breakdown had in fact all been carefully calculated to increase his chances of being resurrected after the hanging. The county physician immediately put the pieces together.

By refusing to eat and pacing endlessly, Cardinella had lost a lot of weight, meaning the fall was less likely to kill him on its own—less weight on the noose meant less chance that the neck would break. Even the breakdown on the scaffold had most likely been a ruse to ensure that he'd be tied in the chair. The noose was not adjusted for the difference, so Cardinella began his drop with a head start: Sitting in the chair, his neck was about a foot and a half lower than it would have been had he been standing. With a shorter drop and lighter weight, there was a good chance Cardinella would strangle to death rather than die of a broken neck. And if his spine was intact, he could, at least in theory, be brought back to life.

McNamara later claimed the first part of the ruse had worked—Cardinella had died of strangulation (though the death certificate lists the cause of death as "fracture of the 2nd cervical vertebrae")—and that if the police hadn't put a stop to the scheme, there was a slim chance the resurrection could have been pulled off. McNamara and a few guards were dispatched to the morgue, where they ran tests on the body to make sure any further attempts to restore life to the body would be fruitless.

"The Devil's" death certificate shows that his planned resurrection would have been impossible. PUBLIC RECORD

Sam Cardinella's body was eventually taken away and buried at Mount Olivet Cemetery. But the mysteries of his gang were still not completely solved.

For instance: Why had he been repeating Viana's name to the family? Where did "The Choir Boy" fit into the plan?

No one knows for sure, but there were whisperings in the underworld for years that eventually got back to the chief physician. Cardinella believed he could be brought back to life because his friends had already tested the procedure on Viana—and it had worked.

According to legend, the always cult-like gang had resorted to magic. Once in the ambulance, Viana's lifeless body was taken to some secret location, where a combination of stimulants, electricity, and other resuscitants had been administered to the body. Strange black-robed "magicians" circled around the body and the doctors, chanting strange incantations in Italian.

The chanting ceased as Viana opened his eyes, and a faint moan was heard from his mouth.

But a rise from the grave, even according to the wildest versions of the legend, was not to be. Viana was, after all, a traitor and could not be allowed to live. The "magicians" let him die again on the table. The resuscitation attempt had never been to bring *him* back to life; it was only an experiment to see if it could be done and then repeated four months later on the gang's ringleader: Sam Cardinella.

No one really knows if this story was true; it was merely whispered among underworld types in the prison for years to come. But Cardinella certainly seems to have *thought* it was true as he was led to his execution.

But even at the time of his death in 1921, Sam Cardinella was becoming an anachronism—the leader of a gang of two-bit thugs practicing holdups against regular civilians. In the very shadow of his pool hall, a new sort of organized crime was rising: the kind that would define Chicago in the eyes of the world for generations to come.

CHAPTER THREE

Big Jim and Johnny the Fox

By the time Sam Cardinella was led to the gallows, he was already a relic of an earlier era. Gangs that worked holdups and Black Hand scams were strictly small potatoes in 1921. Better organized gangs in the levee district around 22nd and Wabash—right in the heart of Cardinella's stomping grounds—were aligning themselves with local government, increasing their power and snuffing the Black Handers out of existence.

In January 1920 the Eighteenth Amendment to the United States Constitution had gone into effect, outlawing the sale and consumption of alcohol in the United States. In the early years it does seem to have had some impact on people's drinking habits; according to some estimates, based on the decrease in deaths from cirrhosis, consumption of hard liquor was cut in half nationwide.

Very few people took the law seriously though, and millions openly flouted it. The National Archives now estimates that there were between thirty thousand and one hundred thousand illegal "speakeasies" in New York City,

A pair of brave men try out the "new stuff" that will "make you want to climb a tree." LIBRARY OF CONGRESS

and an estimate of twenty-five thousand is tossed around for the number of such places in Chicago. It's difficult to tell what the real number was—illegal as they were, most speakeasies didn't generate a lot of paperwork that can be checked today—but it's clear that the number was very high. Some believe that the number of places to drink in Chicago actually tripled during Prohibition.

Indeed, there were plenty of signs that the demand for booze had not subsided much; making it illegal made drinking more of a thrill than ever for some people. Sacramental wines for Holy Communion were still legal, and sales skyrocketed. Winemakers who didn't make the sacred stuff had to switch to producing "grape concentrate," which one would imagine hurt sales. But by the end of the decade, some estimates have it that grape production had increased by 700 percent. Grape dealers had taken to putting warning labels on every bottle stating that unless handled carefully, the juice could ferment. Sales reps cheerfully warned consumers that they'd better not put the grape concentrate into a jug and keep it in a warm place for twenty-one days or it would turn into wine. Some companies sold grapes in concentrated "bricks" with instructions to dissolve the brick in one gallon of water, along with a note saying to add a tenth of a percent of benzoate of soda to "prevent fermentation." Consumers got the message—that if you let it dissolve *without* the benzoate, it would ferment—loud and clear.

But even with wine readily available, the market for beer and the harder stuff continued to be strong. The price of a drink skyrocketed, and gangsters immediately realized that there was a fortune to be made. Running gambling halls, bordellos, and protection rackets, as the levee district gangsters had been doing, seemed like small-time stuff now, and every gangster was ready to get his feet wet.

There was just one thing that stood in their way, and it certainly wasn't the police: Big Jim Colosimo, the most powerful man in the levee underworld, didn't want anything to do with liquor and apparently ordered all the men under his authority to stay away from the stuff.

To most appearances, Colosimo was a respectable pillar of the community, owner of the upscale Colosimo's Cafe on South Wabash, which featured high-end food and opera singers as entertainment. He was even a precinct captain in the First Ward. But the First Ward was a notorious den of brothels and gambling parlors led by Aldermen "Bathhouse" John Coughlin and Michael "Hinky Dink" Kenna. Criminals there operated with something close to immunity, as long as they made all the proper payoffs. Big Jim, ever an entrepreneur, owned plenty of two-bit whorehouses in the levee himself.

You'd never know the area was seedy by the crowd at Colosimo's, though. It had started out as another low-end joint, with piano music provided by a character named "Izzy the Rat," but as Colosimo's fortunes grew, and his tastes became more refined, the food and music in his cafe both improved. The feeling that they were eating among criminals in a hotbed of wickedness and corruption only made the restaurant more attractive to some people. They knew criminals had to behave themselves there, and it became a place where the society set could rub elbows with lowlifes. Big Jim supposedly hosted notables like Al Jolson and Enrico Caruso whenever they were in town.

Colosimo's Enforcer

In his early days, Colosimo had dealt with plenty of minor threats from the Black Hand and had generally paid them off (though some reports have him strangling a couple of the extortionists to death with his bare hands). But the Black Hand could be like a mangy stray dog for business owners—feed them once and they'll never leave you alone. Around 1909 or 1910, he got fed up with their demands and decided to bring in some muscle of his own. So he called in a cousin of his wife, Victoria: a young New Yorker named Johnny Torrio, a major player in the deadly Five Points gang.

Torrio dealt with the extortionists severely. He would make arrangements to pay them off, and when they arrived at an agreed-upon meeting place, he'd pull out his gun. Some of them were scared off; some of them were killed.

Torrio and Colosimo both had experience in running Black Hand rackets of their own so they knew a bit about how they operated. The men who had forced Big Jim to call in an enforcer were particularly ruthless. Clearly not afraid of any legends about his strangling people, they were demanding as much as $50,000 in payouts.

Johnny agreed to meet the men under a viaduct near Clark Street and Archer Avenue, where he tried his best to negotiate. He was a gifted talker, so much so that even his rivals would one day refer to him as "Nice Johnny." But the Black Handers didn't want to negotiate, and Torrio arranged to meet them again the next night to make his payment. The next evening he stood under a streetlight, holding up what appeared to be a satchel full of money. Outside the glare of the streetlight sat a pair of armed thugs.

There was no money in the satchel, but Torrio hadn't come empty-handed—or unarmed. When the thugs stepped into view, he made his move.

According to legend, when Big Jim asked how the meeting went, Torrio simply said, "I looked back, and they didn't wave good-bye."

The other local Black Handers got the message quickly: Big Jim Colosimo was off-limits if you wanted to live. Going after him was too dangerous.

Johnny Torrio had risen through the ranks of the Five Points gang in New York to become an assistant boss with a tough reputation; he had apparently worked with the Lenox Avenue gang alongside such luminaries as Harry "Gyp the Blood" Horowitz and "Lefty Louie" Rosenberg. Rosenberg would eventually become notorious for murdering notable gambler Harold Rosenthal near Times Square in a case that would keep the police—and the *New York Times*—busy for months. Coming into Chicago, he was an ideal bodyguard for Colosimo, and when Big Jim decided he wanted to focus more of his energies on running a fine restaurant and being a legitimate showbiz impresario, the management of most of the seedier joints was given to Torrio.

And Torrio proved himself to be an able businessman.

One of the brothels, the Saratoga, hadn't really been paying off—the top price for a night with one of the girls was only a dollar. It was well known in the brothel

The tomb of Big Jim Colosimo has survived recent break-in attempts. PHOTO BY AUTHOR

world, though, that you didn't necessarily need to raise the quality of services to raise your prices. One place in the levee had a "cheap" entrance and a "high-end" $5 entrance, and both of them led to the same girls.

Torrio hatched a plan: He dressed the girls up in gingham dresses (schoolgirl outfits) and jacked up the prices. Profits soared, even after a personal inspection of the vice district by the mayor got him arrested. Torrio's name was one of seventeen listed in Chicago papers in 1913 as having been arrested for running a bawdy house.

But the investigation of the Saratoga hadn't exactly been thorough enough to cause true trouble. "Of course," Mayor Harrison carefully pointed out, "my observations were from the exterior, but I was convinced that these saloons were flagrant violators of the law. They were brassy in the way that they ignored police regulations. . . . I want [this] to be a notice to the police that I know they have not been doing their work."

These exterior views on their own were not enough evidence to convict anyone. None of the girls would testify against Nice Johnny, either out of admiration for or fear of him (take your pick), and he was soon let go. Colosimo, presumably through his own considerable clout with the local government, managed not to be arrested at all, even though he still technically owned the place. The next year, when new police districts were created, State's Attorney Maclay Hoyne asked the mayor to close a number of saloons, including Colosimo's itself. The mayor simply said that he'd "take it under advisement."

The City versus the Levee

Raids of taverns, gambling dens, and brothels in those days were common, but as the raids above showed, the result was seldom more than newspaper notices that probably served only as free publicity. Police rarely reported anything after a raid. More evidence would come from men like P. O. Florence, who was employed by a pastor to spy on the Medinah Hotel at Chicago and Clark. Florence would rent a room and drill holes in the wall in order to see what was happening in the adjacent rooms.

Rather than providing details of what Florence saw, the papers reported on the testimony he later gave in court. "When his full unexpurgated recollections of nights at the peep hole had gone into the record," wrote the *Tribune*, "it was pretty well established that the moral restraints imposed by the Medinah management on its guests were not oppressive." He was not alone in his peeping; one woman who lived across the street said it was her custom to sit at her window with the lights out and watch the show in the hotel windows.

But State's Attorney Hoyne seemed to have it in for Colosimo and kept pressing his case. Though graft and bribes to the police were common, one man couldn't be bought—Inspector W. C. Dannenberg, the very detective who had raided the Medinah based on the "peeper's" information.

Through Dannenberg's influence, the police chiefs and attorneys were able to keep an eye on what was going on in the levee district, and in summer 1914 a council was held on what to do about it. Raids on the levee were coming back into fashion, to the extent that it was said that the only thing going on in the district was that detectives were driving through to keep an eye on "lookouts" while those same lookouts kept their eyes on the detectives. With so many raids going on, most businesses in the levy were putting up a respectable front. In some the legitimate entertainers—singers and musicians—were coming to outnumber the patrons.

"The levee is on the bum for true," an unnamed barman at 22nd and Wabash told the *Tribune*. "They's no tellin' when things'll be opened up right again."

But though they could no longer find anything disreputable going on, the police weren't satisfied; they knew that 22nd Street was far from clean. Department heads met with Chief of Police Gleason, along with various notables including M. L. C. Funkhouser of the "morality" squad, whose duties included censoring the new moving picture shows of any objectionable material. (He was eventually caught charging people money for private screenings of the naughty bits.)

"There are not enough men in the 22nd Street district to clean up the territory," said Gleason. "Possibly the men there are too well known to be effective."

Gleason had been trying to clean up the levee ever since he took office, and under the Vagrancy Act, he arrested men who could not show that they had any visible means of support. This was a nuisance for many of the vice lords. Since their money was all laundered, they had no visible means of support and could therefore be arrested as vagrants, no matter how high they were living. Most were freed in a day or two, though. Raids or none, the vice lords were operating under the protection of Aldermen "Bathhouse" John Coughlin and Hinky Dink Kenna, who had the chief of the neighborhood police station on their payroll.

Still, "untouchable" Inspector Dannenberg was an effective raider; he once rounded up nearly one hundred vice lords in a single night, which was a pain in the neck even for men who knew they'd be back on the streets in hours. At one point, knowing that Dannenberg was an avid "autoist" who enjoying driving around the city, some shadowy figures parked a new car in front of Dannenberg's house and let it be known that if two of Torrio's places were left alone, the car would be left there. Dannenberg refused, and the car was removed.

As the police and more sympathetic officials worked to fulfill Dannenberg's plans to flush out the levee once and for all, Colosimo and Torrio met with other vice lords and determined to set a trap that would put the inspector out of the way and send a message to anyone else.

On the night of July 16, 1914, several bands of cops were patrolling the area when a mysterious red car pulled up alongside one of them. The men inside of it were armed.

A firefight, soon dubbed "The Battle of the Badlands" by the press, broke out in front of a store, and a mysterious "man in gray" fired a shot that killed a police officer. Several others—cops and bystanders—were injured in the three-minute brawl, including a member of the "gun mob" with the memorable name of Roxy Vanilla. Torrio hustled him into a car and began to transport him back and forth among several hospitals, switching him from one to another as soon as he was identified.

A policeman known only as "Officer 666" took to the papers with an editorial the next day, ready to bare everything he'd learned about the underworld. "I'll tell you the name of the man who was brought here all the way from the Pacific Ocean to get Dannenberg," he said. "I'll tell you why he isn't under arrest. And when I get through, if you are not convinced that there was a deliberate plot to murder the morals inspector and his men . . . I'll give up."

He then recounted how "Johnny Turio [sic], who takes orders from Jim Colosimi [sic]," had been on the scene of the battle and was able to get away with his whole mob in his red car, except that Roxy Vanilla had been winged by the gunfire. Officer 666 knew that cracking the case wouldn't be easy. "Roxy is coached," he explained. "He's

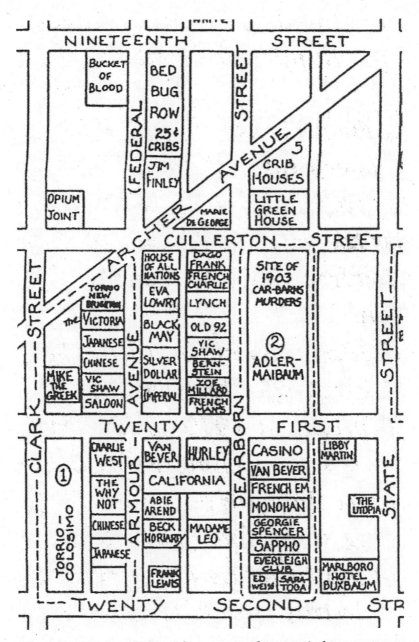

Map of the levee district from an early twentieth-century cop

primed to tell them he went into a store to buy something and got shot, and Johnny Turio will say he was just driving by and picked him up. But it will be hard for Johnny to explain why he picked him up and dashed away, while the dead and injured lay all about."

He went on to specifically name Mack Fitzpatrick, a gangster from San Francisco, as the actual man who had killed a police officer. But the police wouldn't find Fitzpatrick. According to Officer 666's lament, a crooked cop had tipped Fitzpatrick off that the cops knew about him and he'd skipped town.

But though the battle failed to wipe out either the vice lords or the morality squads, it was the morality squads that came out with the upper hand. The death of the police officer led to more outcry against the levee and, as a result, more action. Raids got so common that legend had it that sometimes a squad would raid the front door of a place fully unaware that another squad was coming in through the back. Torrio and most of the other big shots in the area got out of town to cool their heels—nearly all of them, in fact, except Colosimo, who believed himself pretty well above the law.

A New Boss

But the heat cooled down quickly enough. In 1915 a new mayor was elected. William Hale "Big Bill" Thompson was perhaps the most colorful, and ludicrous, mayor ever to serve in Chicago (which is really saying something). Thompson had run on promises to clean up the town but was actually supported by Big Jim Colosimo. Contributions from Colosimo helped elect Thompson, and it seemed odd that a vice lord would align himself with a reformer. When Big Bill took office, Inspector

Dannenberg was fired, and the captain of the 22nd Street station in the heart of the levee was transferred out of the district and replaced with men more willing to look the other way for the right price.

With all the most-effective raiders out of the scene, the levee flourished again. In those days it was widely believed (by men like Thompson) that if you had one "red light district" in which to concentrate all the crime and vice, the rest of the city would be cleaner.

Still, even with a mayor in office who didn't seem to care about the levee, bribes had to be paid to keep things running smoothly; even as Torrio came back to town, Colosimo dutifully paid good money to the police chief for protection. In 1917 a man testified that Colosimo had been paying $100 a month to an agent who delivered it directly to Chief Healey. All told, the payments the informant had taken from Colosimo made up about 10 percent of the nearly $14,000 he had collected for the chief.

In this same testimony, it became clear that Torrio had been branching out from under Colosimo's wing, ready to go into business for himself.

During his testimony at Healey's 1917 graft trial, Thomas Costello, who described himself as the head of a veritable police bribery syndicate, was asked if he knew a man named John Torrio.

"Yes, sir," he said. "It was my understanding that he ran a chain of disorderly houses. . . . He came into my office and told me that Police Captain Smith of Twenty-second Street had sent him down to see me. He said that he understood that I was friendly with the chief . . . and he wanted to have some places of his own and his friends taken care of so that the police would not interfere with them."

Costello went straight to Captain Healy and said that Torrio was offering $400 a month.

"I don't like to handle that money; that's pretty hot," Healey reportedly said. "I will tell you what I will do, Tom. You take the money, and I will look after it for you."

"Much obliged to you," Costello had replied. "I will."

Torrio met up with Costello at the Studebaker Theatre and got into his car; the men embarked on a tour of six places Torrio wanted to protect from police interference around the levee. Torrio gave him one envelope for each of the places, and Costello put them into his overcoat pocket without a word.

Having learned a few lessons from vice raids, Torrio had decided that keeping everything in one neighborhood made it too easy for the police to know where to find you. Hence he began to expand his own empire, first out from under Colosimo's watch, then outside the levee district, and then outside Chicago itself. Acting on a tip, he invested in a two-story building eighteen miles south of downtown, right on the Indiana border. He bought it for a song, installed a bar, and stocked the bedrooms with girls imported right from the levee. The girls alone were said to bring in about nine grand a month, and Torrio used the money to open up a whole string of other seedy joints.

Burnham, Indiana, where Torrio soon controlled a little kingdom, was said to have "more whores per square foot" than any other town in the world. But Torrio established his headquarters right back in the levee, around the corner from Colosimo's Cafe, at 2222 South Wabash, in a four-story building he called the Four Deuces. There was a bar on the first floor, a bordello on the fourth, and gambling rooms in the middle floors.

But vice was all just business to Torrio. By all accounts, "Nice Johnny" stayed away from girls, gambling, and drinks. He set up a house for himself down on 64th Street, far away from the levee, and was so devoted to his wife that it was said she had no idea he was involved in any kind of shady business.

Keeping up this charade required Torrio to be away from his establishments in the evening, when the joints were really hopping. To look after the Four Deuces, Torrio brought in a young bodyguard and doorman named Alphonse Capone.

The Death of Big Jim

Colosimo, meanwhile, was still technically the boss, and he was settling into a life of ease. He divorced his first wife in March 1920, just as Prohibition was getting under way, and married Dale Winter, a pretty young singer whom locals took to referring to as "Little Mrs. Big Jim." With aid and encouragement from the likes of opera star Enrico Caruso, Colosimo enrolled his pretty young wife in the Chicago Musical College and began to push her career as a singer hard. Soon he was a legend in his own mind, a showbiz star maker who also happened to be famous in his own right. Diners would applaud the happy couple when they paraded through the elegant nightclubs of Michigan Avenue. He wore several diamond rings—diamonds were always a good investment, and the flashy Big Jim adored them.

But Torrio had advised against the divorce and remarriage. Colosimo's first wife, Victoria, a former madam, wasn't a woman to be trifled with, and her brothers were concerned that their futures wouldn't be as bright if they weren't in-laws to the notorious Big Jim. They wouldn't take his desertion of Victoria lightly.

Of the marriage, Torrio is said to have told Jim, "It's your funeral."

By this time liquor was illegal, and John Torrio, for one, smelled money. There was a fortune to be made selling the stuff illegally. The government couldn't legislate the public demand for booze out of existence any more than anti-prostitution laws could take away the appetites of the flesh.

But Colosimo was putting his foot down. He told Torrio to stick to the women—that was where the money was, after all. Bootlegging liquor was going to be small-time stuff. Prohibition would never last.

It's hard to imagine that Colosimo really believed this. Any fool could see that mixing bootleg liquor was going to be like printing your own money for as long as Prohibition held. But Torrio couldn't simply part ways with his boss, even as his own empire was expanding. As Hymie Weiss, a later gang kingpin, summed it up: "Once you're in with us, you're in for life."

Maybe Torrio decided that it was time to move on, and that expanding into the wider world of bootlegging would only be possible if Big Jim Colosimo was out of the way. Maybe some of the former in-laws wanted revenge on Big Jim. Perhaps some of the friends of Black Handers he'd put out of business had marked him for death.

In any case, Big Jim's days were numbered.

He was married on April 20, 1920. On May 11, only three weeks later, he was dead.

At 4:30 that day he had come into his cafe to take care of some business. After talking with some book-keepers in the back room, he went out toward the lobby. It was there that two shots were fired at him. One bullet shattered the glass that surrounded a vacant cashier's station; the other went right into Colosimo's head. He had been armed himself of course, but he never had a chance to reach for his own gun. By the time he landed, face down, he was already a dead man.

A short while later, following a massive funeral, Colosimo was laid to rest in a family mausoleum at Oak Woods Cemetery on the South Side. In 2012 an attempted break-in (allegedly by people who believed he was buried in a solid gold casket) left the door mangled and the interior visible. Anyone with a camera that could be stuck into the door could get a shot of the huge stone slab covering his vault, on which the words JAMES COLOSIMO were carved above the dates 1871–1919.

This created a bit of a mystery. Why did the slab say 1919 when Big Jim was killed in 1920?

But that was far from the only mystery that surrounded the big man's death, or the most important. The slayer ran away after the shooting, and there were no solid witnesses. When asked if she suspected anyone, Little Mrs. Big Jim could say only, "I should say I suspect *everyone.*"

Police had no real clues, except for some evidence that this was no random robbery. Big Jim had been wearing his usual array of diamonds, and none of these were taken. The only other clue was a note addressed to Colosimo, found in the cafe. It read, "Deaths are dancing with deaths."

Plenty of men were rounded up and arrested, but none of the charges against them ever stuck. But rumors went around that the triggerman had been one of the tougher guys from Torrio's operation: the one they all called Scarface Al.

Maybe it wasn't Al Capone—maybe no one ever truly believed it was. But the hit on Big Jim seemed to give Capone a reputation that would help him in his climb to the top over the next few years, when the money available from bootleg beer made girls and gambling seem like chump change and Black Hand operations became a thing of the past.

CHAPTER FOUR

The Beer Wars of '23

In 1920 the *Chicago Tribune* employed an "inquiring photographer" who would ask five random people a question on the street. The feature was first run on September 2, 1920, only eight months after Prohibition came into effect, and the question of the day was "How does the new booze compare with the old?" Only one of the five people hanging around Clark Street near Austin (now Hubbard) that day denied having been drinking in the previous months (and even that guy seemed to have more firsthand knowledge than he let on), but none of the men were enthusiastic about the quality of bootleg liquor, as can be seen from their quotes:

> "There's a fight in every pint and a murder in a gallon. I used to drink the old stuff, but I'll tell the world I leave the new alone."
>
> —*J. W. Gibson, salesman*

"I liked the old stuff better. It was much cheaper and you didn't feel so bum the next a.m. The only difference I see is that they've raised the price of headaches."

—*J. W. Johnson, chief vault clerk*

"You could take a half dozen shots of the old stuff and never feel it. If you take two drinks of the new booze, it's good-bye, George."

—*Harry Brown, broker*

"The effect is altogether different, judging by the stories I read in the papers. I would say the new booze excites a man to do things he never would have done under the influence of the old."

—*John Schmidt, investigator*

"Because they can't get it they want it all the more. The new stuff is causing more deaths every day. It knocks you off your feet, and after taking a half dozen shots you want to climb a tree."

—*M. Winsberg, saloon proprietor*

The very fact that one of these men identified himself as a saloon proprietor probably speaks volumes about how openly the law was flouted; surely no one thought that all the saloons still in operation were just serving tea and soda.

Clearly, though, the demand for alcohol was there, and the gangsters knew it. The problem they faced was how to keep up a supply to sell to the saloonkeepers. Some of them had it smuggled in from Canada, but that was a risky operation, not to mention a costly one. The booze the men in the "Inquiring Photographer" feature had been consuming was probably more of the "bathtub gin" variety: homemade booze mixed together with all sorts of ingredients—everything up to and including embalming fluid—mixed in to give it a kick. Some of these ingredients were poisonous and could lead to symptoms far worse than a desire to climb a tree, including blindness, psychosis, even death, but a bit of glycerin added in made it just smooth enough to swallow. The smoothness didn't make it any safer, though; some estimate that over the years, bad booze killed more people than the gangsters did.

To a gangster of means, the easiest way to get decent liquor in large supply was simply to buy a working brewery. Before Prohibition, the city was full of local breweries, which now were faced with a choice between closing down or changing their production to focus on "near beer," the nonalcoholic stuff—the sort of drink my friends refer to as "pee water."

There was also "hidden" option #3: They could go into business with men like Johnny Torrio.

Torrio made deals with several breweries in town. Sometimes he bought them outright; sometimes he just agreed to act as a "front." They'd continue brewing just as they'd done before, only now they'd make beer for one client—Torrio—and he'd take the blame if anything happened. Soon his breweries were pumping out hundreds of gallons of proper beer every day.

Johnny the Fox and Scarface Al

Johnny Torrio, by now referred to as both "Nice Johnny" and "Johnny the Fox," may have been the greatest criminal mastermind the city every produced. Lots of men died because they were on the wrong side of him, but somehow he never seemed to get his own hands dirty. He personally didn't like fighting, and it was said that he never carried a gun after graduating from his days as Colosimo's enforcer. He ran some of the city's slickest vice operations but didn't indulge in the products he sold or the "entertainment" at the resorts he owned. He ran his operations just as though they were any other business, and every night he went home to his wife, who described their marriage as "one long, unclouded honeymoon."

By many accounts the man didn't even swear; a "respectable friend" of reporter James O'Donnell Bennett who knew Torrio fairly well said, "I never heard him utter a profane or lewd word. He loves music—loves to take apart phrases and motives in the score of an opera—singing them to illustrate the points he is making. He does not like to talk shop, as [north side mobster Dean] O'Banion did. He was no night roisterer. At six o'clock he would go home to supper in his flat—and he would stay there."

It was during his nine-to-six life that he created one of the most notorious criminal empires the world would ever know.

It was Torrio, more than anyone else, who turned the levee organizations from loose networks of thugs and pimps and bodyguards into an "outfit." It wasn't yet a Mafia in the New York sense of the word; there were no rituals for joining, no blood oaths or anything of that sort. There were no shadowy old men from old countries calling the shots. This was a new kind of outfit.

Unlike some other mobs of the day, membership wasn't even based on national origin. People retelling the story of Chicago gangs today often say the Torrio-Capone gangs of the South Side were Italian while the North Side gang run by Dean O'Banion was Irish, and that much of the conflict was due to racial prejudice. This is sort of a partial truth but more of an oversimplification.

The O'Banion gang was *mainly* Irish but had a few Italians in the ranks. The Torrio crowd was largely men of Neapolitan descent, but they had plenty of members who were from nowhere close to Italy, and they worked closely with the Unione Siciliana, the fraternal organization of Sicilians that had tried to stamp out the Black Hand a decade before. Somewhere along the line, as the Unione had grown in power, they had been taken over by men who kept a hand in the world of organized crime and wielded considerable influence over the gangs. Of the major groups, however, the only one from Sicily was the Genna Brothers, who operated in the neighborhood known as Little Italy.

Young Al Capone—known as "Scarface" only behind his back—quickly rose through the ranks and took over the management of the Four Deuces club on Wabash and even brought in a protégé of his own: Frank Nitti, who would come to be known as "Frank the Enforcer."

Capone was something of a loose cannon in those days, to say the least. In August 1922 he was driving around drunk and crashed his car into a parked taxicab at Randolph and Wabash. Rather than drive away, Capone came roaring out of the car, waving a revolver in one hand and a sheriff's deputy badge in another, threatening to shoot a witness who said the crash was his fault.

The next day the *Tribune* reported that "Alfred Caponi" had been arrested. (They would persist in calling him "Al Caponi" for years.)

"Alfred Caponi, alleged owner of the 'Four Deuces,' a brothel at 2222 Wabash Avenue, will face three charges," they said. He had been arrested for "assault with an automobile, driving while intoxicated and carrying concealed weapons." He was taken to the Central Station, where he declared that he could have the arresting officer fired. As they locked him up for the night, he promised that his "pull" would make their life difficult and said, "I'll fix this thing so easy you won't know how it's done."

He was quickly bailed out and never returned to court on the charge. But had Capone kept operating with that attitude and demeanor, it's doubtful he would have lasted long in the outfit. Torrio, though, taught him a better way of doing business. Capone would always be rougher, more paranoid, and more of a hedonist than Torrio, but Torrio taught him the difference between saying "We don't want any trouble" and "Are you looking for trouble?"

And it was probably Torrio's pull, not Capone's, that got young Scarface out of trouble after his drunk driving escapades.

Building an Empire

Beyond a doubt, Torrio was paying the police handsomely. The police didn't like the Prohibition laws any more than anyone else, and many were only too happy to take bribes to look the other way during inspections of the breweries. Sometimes the beer trucks that delivered products from the breweries to the saloons even had police escorts.

Torrio was, in fact, paying several people off as he expanded his empire out into the suburbs. When he wanted to put up a new establishment, cooperation of the neighbors was key, and Torrio made it worth their while. He's said to have paid their mortgages, bought them cars, and even sent men to repair leaking roofs. None of this came cheap, but it was a small price to pay for his burdening the neighbors with a "resort" that might employ as many as sixty prostitutes on their block.

Anyway, he could afford it—his prostitution rings were making him something in the neighborhood of $100,000 a year (roughly three million in today's money). By 1925 the bootleg liquor would be making him tens of millions. Soon the brothels seemed to exist mainly to give people a place where they could also buy Torrio's booze.

These places were rigged up carefully. Most were set off on side roads and connected to gas stations by electric wires. If a detail of "honest" cops was seen passing the gas station, a lookout stationed there would sound an alarm on the wires. By the time the cops arrived, the booze and the girls would be gone.

Torrio's was, in many ways, a rags to riches story right out of a dime novel. He had come to the United States at the age of two and spent his childhood working hard, pulling himself up by his bootstraps. Details as to exactly what *kind* of work he'd done are a bit vague today. He himself was not above changing the story, but he seems to have worked as a delivery boy, a boxing promoter, and a handful of other jobs. It was as a boxing promoter that he got roped into gang work and learned of the money to be made in rigging boxing matches.

But though he surely learned a thing or two about violence in those days, with all the money to be made in bootleg liquor, he saw no reasons for the gangs to be fighting anymore. "There are millions in booze," he reportedly said. "Plenty for everyone. All we gotta do is respect the other guy's area and we'll make money."

He pulled around eight of the biggest local gangs into his organization and talked them into stopping all the small-time stuff—no more holdups, no more safecracking, no more jewelry heists that might alert the authorities. From here on out, they'd just work in the semirespectable field of manufacturing and delivering alcohol (and running houses of ill repute—that was still all right). And so it was that the city was divided up into territories. The Torrio-Capone gang got a wide swath of the South Side, and much of the North Side (minus the lucrative Gold Coast) went to Dean O'Banion.

Other territories went to the Genna Brothers, the Saltis-McErlane gang, and others. Soon Torrio had a fleet of as many as eight hundred gunmen working for him. He felt that he had no need to carry a gun himself and often walked around the city without a personal bodyguard.

Amazingly, this loose affiliation of gangsters worked out reasonably well for the first few years of the 1920s. Several members of different gangs were even living in the Congress Hotel at the same time. The most notable break in the truce was a flare-up in 1923 that came to be known as the Beer Wars—both for the war the Feds waged against the beer and the battle between rival beer gangs that broke out that year, setting the stage for the war that would soon consume the city.

The Warning Shots of the Great War

Torrio's organization was a slick one, but with so many rough men under the umbrella, flare-ups were inevitable. Not all the gangsters were going to share his philosophy that "there's plenty for everyone," and some of these men were just not going to be content with a life of running beer trucks, no matter how well it paid.

And Torrio hadn't succeeded in making room for everyone who wanted in.

In the early 1920s there were two O'Donnell gangs in the city. On the northwest side of the city was the Klondike O'Donnell gang, part of Torrio's syndicate. But Torrio had failed to make any provisions for the other

O'Donnells, the Spike O'Donnell gang, which operated on the South Side. When the city was divided up, Spike O'Donnell was serving time in prison in Joliet, and Torrio doesn't seem to have thought the other three O'Donnell brothers were worthy of his consideration. Spike was an accomplished criminal. Although a devout Catholic who went to Mass regularly (as the gangsters almost always did), he had twice been on trial for murder and was an ace burglar. His brothers were little more than two-bit thugs, and with their elder brother and leader incarcerated, all they could do was hang around in Torrio's clubs, hoping to be given a bit of work here and there.

But when Spike got out of prison and took his place at the head of his brothers, Torrio still didn't cut them into the action. Spike decided they would take things into their own hands. The Spike O'Donnell gang began to hijack trucks carrying Torrio beer and even tried to make inroads into controlling the supply of booze at a few choice saloons. To get saloons to switch to them from other gangs, they started sending thugs into saloons to ask, "Who do you buy your beer from?" If the answer was not favorable to the Spike O'Donnell gang, the thug might give the saloonkeeper a very, very good reason to change suppliers, with help from the blunt end of a gun.

Obviously Torrio couldn't let this stand—nor could the gangs who had controlled the saloons the O'Donnells were trying to take over. On September 7, 1923, things between the gangs got rough.

On that day the O'Donnell brothers were taking care of business in a saloon at 5358 South Lincoln Street. There were already indications that there was trouble on the horizon; Steve O'Donnell had gone to the police station to report that five men in a car had tried to rob him outside his house of the payroll to pay his ten teams of drivers. "I pulled a gun and fired one shot, and they blew," he said.

The police were a bit puzzled—they knew Steve O'Donnell was a part of his brother Spike's gang. Why would such a man ask for police protection? Something fishy was going on for sure. When O'Donnell left, the police determined to find where his brothers were and what they were up to.

Later that day, three members of the Spike O'Donnell gang were in a saloon on West 51st Street, trying to strong-arm the proprietor, Jacob Geis, into stocking O'Donnell beer. The argument ended with Geis being knocked about the head with the handles of several guns, all in front of six customers. One of the customers tried to intervene and was knocked out for his trouble. The O'Donnells fled the scene, and the two wounded men were taken to a hospital, where Geis languished in critical condition for some time. (He would survive, but his troubles were far from over; a decade later his place would be bombed in the continuing gang war.)

Later that same night, two Spike O'Donnell gangsters were settling down to dinner at Klepka's saloon accompanied by Jerry O'Connor, one of their beer runners, when four men came tearing through the door, three with revolvers and one with a shotgun. One of the men was Frank McErlane, of the Saltis-McErlane gang, whose saloons they'd been muscling into.

"Now give us a square deal," shouted one of the men, presumably McErlane. "Come outside and fight it out."

And with that, he began to shoot.

The O'Donnells tried to escape the hail of bullets through the back door of the saloon. By the time the four Saltis-McErlane men got back into their car and sped away, Jerry O'Connor had been shot through the heart. He was dead on arrival at a nearby doctor's office.

The beer war had begun.

And not just the war among the beer gangs—an official "war on beer" was breaking out in the city at the same time.

Bootlegging had certainly flourished under the "leadership" of Mayor Big Bill Thompson, who seemed to get loopier, lazier, and more corrupt by the day during his term. But in 1923 there was a new mayor in town, William Dever, who promised to clean up the city. He sympathized with people who wanted to drink. He said he fondly hoped Prohibition would soon end and that the people of Chicago could again access "wholesome" beer at fair prices, but he insisted that this could never happen until the bootleggers were out of business. Voters seemed to agree; he was elected in a landslide.

Chicago officials tried their best to make liquor legal again. In June 1923 local aldermen voted 37–8 on a resolution stating that "light wines" and beer should be allowed and sent a plea to Congress to modify the federal laws. However, Prohibition was still the law of the land, written into the Constitution by the Eighteenth Amendment. No local resolution could bring it down unless the Constitution was amended again, and that was no easy task, even for a sympathetic and effective Congress. And whoever heard of an "effective Congress"?

The meeting at which the aldermen made the resolution was as far out of control as any congressional session, with much shouting throughout. A vocal "dry" faction tried to kill the resolution, but it was saved when "Bathhouse" John Coughlin made a "motion to reconsider." Mayor Dever was referring to the rowdy meeting when he repeatedly beat his gavel and said, "We can't do business amid such disorder," but he could have been speaking about the city itself.

Meanwhile, Dever was promising to stamp out the graft in the police department that kept the beer runners safe from arrest. And in September 1923 he formally opened a war on beer.

The first "battle" into which he sent his men was a huge embarrassment for him, though. On September 14 police officers under his command staged raids at several breweries, expecting to find that the workers there were brewing real beer, not "near beer," and rounded up sixty barrels.

But the gangsters must have known the raids were coming—the barrels contained no alcohol, only "fizz."

The newspapers knew perfectly well what was happening. The real beer had been moved to garages and other "strategic parts of town, each controlled by the syndicate chief assigned to that district." The beer was still out there; the syndicates were just smart enough to keep it someplace less obvious than the actual brewery when the mayor was threatening raids. Thirsty citizens had no reason to panic. The *Tribune* noted, "The price of real beer in the loop had not risen yesterday, and there is no appreciable decrease in the supply."

But the mayor and the chief of police remained steadfast in their goal of putting the bootleggers out of business. "Every suspected brewery will be kept tight through the coming week," said Chief Collins on September 16. "There will be no letdown in our vigilance." Every available resource, he said, would be used to find the hiding places where the bootleggers were storing their illicit goods. Guards were placed at the gates of every brewery in town.

However, a war far bigger than the government's was bubbling up to the surface: the war among the gangs themselves. In picking on the Saltis-McErlane gang, the O'Donnell brothers had picked the wrong man to mess with. Frank McErlane was a brutal man, to say the least, and said to be the first Chicago gangster to utilize a Thompson submachine gun. Credited with inventing the "one way ride," he had made a name for himself helping Earl Dear, a condemned young playboy who thought he was above the law because he was friends with gangsters, escape from prison. (Dear was eventually recaptured and hanged.) Coming into power on his own, McErlane got into the habit of stumbling into bars and ordering everyone present to drink with him. He would have two guns with him to make sure everyone played along.

With men like this in positions of power, a war was probably inevitable. Even Torrio's magnificent skills as an organizer couldn't keep men like Frank McErlane tame for long.

The Guns of Frank McErlane

The very next day after Chief Collins's pronouncement, George Meeghan and Spot Butcher, two men from the Spike O'Donnell gang, were sitting in a Ford roadster at Laflin Street and Garfield Boulevard when another car drove by. A man in the other car leaned out the window with a machine gun and riddled the roadster with slugs. Both men inside of it were killed. Later reports said that it hadn't been a drive-by at all; the two men had been captured, bound, and "taken for a ride," though this goes against contemporary accounts that Meeghan had been driving at the time. Several witnesses saw the green car pull up next to the two; one man was driving, and two more, both with guns, were in the backseat.

"It was all done quicker than you could think," one witness said. "The men in the [roadster] probably never saw the men who shot them."

In any case, both men were killed. As the *Tribune* summed it up a year later, "Spot Butcher quit driving a beer truck at the insistence of bullets."

That the shooters were part of Torrio's organization barely needed to be said, but the witness was able to note the license plate of the getaway car: 697 390, which connected the car to John Kane of 7038 South Sangamon. That was also the address of "Paddy" Kane, who had been involved with another gangster, Mossy Enright, some years before. In the 1910s Mossy had led a gang of enforcers for the plumber's union and had cracked a few skulls in addition to shooting a few men to death. He had been a major rival of Big Jim Colosimo.

In the midst of a political struggle as Prohibition first went into effect, Enright had made an attempt on the life of one of Colosimo's men. In retaliation, as Enright drove home from his office in the loop on February 4, 1920, he was tailed by "Sunny Jim" Cosmano. (Cosmano had taken a bullet from Torrio and his men back in his days as a Black Hander but now worked with Colosimo.) As Enright pulled his car over to park, Cosmano shot him twice with a sawed-off shotgun. Enright died in his car.

But memories lingered, even more than three years later, and police assumed that the brother of any friend of Enright was probably linked to a gang of some sort.

In the aftermath of the Meeghan-Butcher killing, several beer runners were rounded up and held by police. Torrio made an appearance at a state's attorney's office, where he denied any complicity in either beer running or any slayings and was not held.

Joseph Butcher, Spot's brother, went to the cops and began to squawk. He told them that for the previous four months he had been working as a beer runner, driving around in a covered wagon containing twenty barrels of the stuff at a time for the Spike O'Donnell gang. The job had gotten dangerous, and he was bitter about it. The bullet that killed his brother, he believed, had been meant for him.

"Every bozo in this town wants to guzzle a glass of real beer without hearing the angels sing," he said, "but it's the poor gink who runs the stuff that gets the bullet through his noodle. Me? I'm through. I wouldn't peddle orange pop at a Sunday school picnic."

In a long interview he laid bare the basics of the O'Donnell operation, saying that he got $50 a week for his services.

"Sure, I'd collect once a week," he said. "Never in the open. Say, this game isn't played under the arc light at the corner of State and Madison, you know. I'd go to [Spike] O'Donnell's house or he'd come to mine. But fifty per's all that ever scratched my fist." He had not served in the recent world war but was confident that beer running was more dangerous than being a soldier. He declared his intention to leave Chicago and head for California— as long as Spike O'Donnell wasn't going there too—right after his brother's funeral.

The O'Donnell brothers, now named in the press as bootleggers in addition to having gangsters shooting at them, scattered to avoid arrest, and police launched a massive manhunt trying to round up the rest of the gang. The gangsters did a better job of finding the O'Donnells than the police did.

In December 1923 two members of the Spike O'Donnell gang, "Morrie" Keane and "Shorty" Egan, were driving one of the O'Donnell beer wagons down Sag Road in south suburban Lemont when they were forced to the side of the road by a blue car. William Channell of the Saltis-McErlane gang was driving; McErlane was in the front seat beside him with a sawed-off shotgun. Keane and Egan were pulled from the car, tied up, and then loaded into the backseat of the blue car.

"Where are you gonna get rid of these guys?" Channell asked Frank as they drove away.

"I'll take care of that in a minute," said McErlane with a laugh. Without another word he turned around and fired his shotgun into Keane's side, waited a second for him to writhe around, then shot him again. Then he fired a shot into Egan's side, another into his leg, and a third into his other side.

McErlane then climbed into the backseat of the moving car, opened the door, and shoved both men out of the car. Keane didn't live long enough to make it to the hospital after the bullet-riddled bodies were found; he was dead on arrival. Egan survived, despite half his face being blown off, and told the authorities the whole story of what had happened.

McErlane was arrested but eventually released, as were most killers in cases like this.

The O'Donnell clan continued making attacks on the Saltis-McErlane gang and their saloons for the next year or so before Walter O'Donnell himself was killed in June 1925. In September of that year, a man presumed to be Frank McErlane made an attempt on Spike O'Donnell's life with a machine gun—some say it was the first time such a weapon was used in a Chicago gang war. Spike and his brother Tom were attacked again the next month in a massive firefight with the Saltis-McErlane gang in Evergreen Park. By 1926 the Spike O'Donnell gang was merely a nuisance, no longer a major threat to anyone else's operations.

The O'Donnell gang continued to make trouble, but Spike, their leader, seems to have settled down somewhat. In 1930 he announced that he was leaving Chicago to pursue an acting career, claiming that he had been offered a fortune to play a gangster in movies. In 1934 he was in London giving lectures on organized crime. He was claiming by then to be the most shot-at gangster in the world; he would eventually go legit as an oil executive and die of natural causes in 1962.

But he would be one of only a few of Chicago's gangsters to die in bed at a ripe old age. The attempts on his life by various gangsters aligned with Torrio were only the beginning of the great gang wars.

While the war was going on, Torrio himself went on vacation, taking his mother on a trip to Italy. While he was away, he supposedly deposited millions into Swiss bank accounts. His organization was kept running in his absence by the capable hands of young Al Capone.

CHAPTER FIVE

The End of the Alliance

Throughout the Beer War of 1923, another battle was heating up. There was a slow rivalry cooking between Torrio and another gang—the gang led by Dean O'Banion, which had been given control of the lower North Side.

O'Banion was a fellow whom people seemed to love and hate at the same time. He was likable, by all accounts; a happy-go-lucky guy who would call you a "swell fellow" on the morning of the day he planned to kill you. And why not? There was no point in being mean to someone in the last hours of his life. Besides, acting unfriendly toward an intended victim might make him suspicious, making the job that much harder.

But just because everyone liked him didn't mean they didn't want the guy dead. Business was business.

O'Banion was a product of Little Hell, growing up there in the days when it was transitioning from an Irish neighborhood into an Italian and Sicilian one. He first appeared in the papers in 1909, listed as the son of Charles O'Banion, who had made the news by climbing up three flights of stairs after being stabbed three times. When young Dean, then working as a milk delivery boy, woke up to go on his route, he found his father lying in a pool of blood in the living room and notified the police. That his first act in the press was asking the police for help would soon come to seem rather ironic.

He got his start as a criminal picking pockets while working as a singing waiter at the McGovern Brothers' restaurant on Clark Street, which would eventually become a dangerous jazz club. (In the early 1980s it would become a punk club named O'Banion's in Dean's honor. It's known as The Kerryman today.) From there he got involved in some of the usual stuff—safecracking, holdups, and robbery.

As an organizer and businessman, he was no John Torrio; but Chief of Police Morgan Collins once called O'Banion "Chicago's arch criminal." It was estimated that he had played a role in the killings of a couple dozen people, either by ordering their death or pulling the trigger himself.

The simple life of running beer around didn't really suit O'Banion in the first place; he was more interested in the exciting world of hijacking and safecracking. Running beer felt like a normal job by comparison—one that paid well, sure, but a job like any other. When the Genna Brothers gang began moving into his territory, it's possible that he was glad to have a reason to fight again.

Certainly by this time O'Banion had an impressive array of gunmen under his own control.

One of the men was Henry Earl Wojciechowski, better known as "Hymie Weiss" or "Hymie the Pole" (whose name alone indicates that it's not entirely accurate to think of the North Siders as an "Irish gang"). The police had once known him as the "perfume burglar" after an escapade in which he knocked over a shelf of sweet-smelling toilet water in the process of robbing the place. He was a dark man who kept to himself and was known to make a lot of loud threats. Perhaps all we need to know about him can be learned from his brother's statement, made in 1926, that "I've seen him once in twenty years . . . that was when he shot me."

Then there was George "Bugs" Moran. "Bugs" was a slang term for "insane" in those days, and like many gangsters, Moran hated his nickname. Say the name in front of him and you'd come to regret it. Raised in St. Paul during an era in which that town was known as a haven for criminals, Moran had gotten his start in Chicago's gangland by holding delivery horses for ransom.

Perhaps the most colorful of them all was Vinnie "The Schemer" Drucci, who was given to dressing up as a priest and wandering around the streets of downtown Chicago, chomping cigars. When a couple walked by, he would say, "Nice ass." When the shocked woman turned to look at him, he would say, "Not you, honey. The fellow!"

The "Moran-O'Banion-Weiss clique," as the papers sometimes called them, had worked together since before Prohibition. In 1918 they were believed to have stolen some $10,000 from the safes of five companies, including those of Standard Oil and Borden's Dairy. One time the police busted them in the middle of a safecracking job, shortly after the first blast had gone off. The men claimed they'd been eating chocolate éclairs next door and had run in when they heard the noise. The jury was convinced, and they went free.

O'Banion's Luck

O'Banion was something of a hero to North Side Chicagoans by then. Though gangsters might have privately hated him, the public had come to see him as something of a Robin Hood–type character, and the threats of what he might do to anyone who messed with his customers seemed to make the area safer. He walked around town with a noticeable swagger. Far from the impoverished child of Little Hell, he was now a wealthy man living in a huge apartment with the pretty girl he had married the year before. As per the typical fashion of gangsters, his wife was said to be completely unaware of his illegal dealings and truly believed that his day job as co-owner of Schofield's Flowers, across from Holy Name Cathedral on State Street, was how he made his living.

But in practice he was as brutal as they came and seemed to be untouchable. In 1921 a man named John Mahoney was arrested for possession of unlawful fire-arms and implicated the "clique" in the theft of alcohol from a company that manufactured it—legally—for use in vanilla extracts. Mahoney's body, dead from a gunshot wound, was found near 18th and Peoria. O'Banion was suspected but never arrested.

In January 1924 O'Banion and a few other men— mostly hangers-on—went to the opening night of a play called *Give and Take* at the La Salle Theatre in the Loop. On the way in, one of his companions told him that Davy Miller, whom they had just met in the lobby with some friends, had insulted him somehow. When the play ended, O'Banion confronted Miller and asked what he had meant by the insult.

Miller denied having made the insult (and was prob-ably telling the truth), but O'Banion continued trying to pick a fight. Miller apparently said, "Let it go; I could lick all three of you with my fists, but not here."

One of O'Banion's companions passed him a gun, and O'Banion shot Davy and Davy's brother Maxie right in front of one thousand theatergoers. Maxie was only hit in the belt buckle, but Davy was wounded badly; he was rushed to the hospital while O'Banion fled. Miller was in critical condition for days before recovering; he never, ever told authorities that it was O'Banion who shot him.

Police knew it was O'Banion from witnesses, though. Two days later they caught him while he and a few others were "peacefully" hijacking a truck containing $30,000 worth of whiskey. O'Banion and Hymie Weiss were both taken in, though the truck got away. (When police found themselves with a choice of either chasing the truck or the limo carrying O'Banion, they went for O'Banion.) He was immediately named by Maxie Miller as the man who shot at him, but somehow O'Banion was never convicted. The man seemed to have golden luck.

Only six weeks later, he would get away with murder again.

The murder in question was that of John Duffy, one of O'Banion's own men in the North Side mob. Whether he was truly part of the gang or just a hanger-on depends on whom you ask, but it seems that O'Banion had given him a few tasks to complete over the years.

Duffy married a girl named Maybelline in February 1924. The marriage was to be a brief one; just over a week after the wedding, the two engaged in a violent, drunken argument. The details of what happened are in dispute (some say he killed her because she dared him to), but Duffy seems to have smothered his bride to death with a pillow, as well as possibly shooting her in the head a couple times, before passing out in a drunken stupor. It's also possible that other gangsters did the deed while Duffy was passed out and arranged the scene to make him think he'd done it himself when he came to.

When he woke up to see what he'd done, Duffy panicked and called for Dean, who arranged to meet him at the Four Deuces, the Capone-Torrio headquarters down in the levee on 22nd Street. Several witnesses saw Duffy go into the Four Deuces. One witness saw him get into a Studebaker (some said it was Al Capone's car) with O'Banion and another man. That was the last time anyone saw Duffy alive.

Duffy had apparently told Davy Miller's other brother, Hirshie, that he'd kill O'Banion if he'd just say the word. Miller, weary of killings already, said no, and a witness to the offer was sworn to secrecy. But the witness seems to have talked to O'Banion, and when Duffy's body was found in a snow bank outside the city, oozing blood from three bullet holes, everyone in town assumed that O'Banion was the killer.

A warrant for O'Banion's arrest was issued, and the *Tribune* headline screamed that the police were hunting "O'Bannion [*sic*], Man of Flowers." Al Capone, also said to be a suspect, walked right into the state's attorney's office and gave a statement that he never knew Duffy and hadn't seen O'Banion in over a month.

"I am a respectable businessman," Capone said. "I do not own or have any connection with the Four Deuces. I own a furniture store adjoining the place, and for no real reason at all somebody is always trying to drag me into something." Clearly, Capone's skills as a PR man had grown tremendously in the two years since his drunk-driving escapades on Wabash.

The hunt for O'Banion was an eventful one. Police traced him to the Congress Hotel, ever a favorite of gangsters, but found another gangster in the room they thought was his. The grinning man gave them a cryptic tip about the *Wolverine Limited,* a passenger train that was leaving at 10 a.m.; the police raided the train but didn't find Dean.

O'Banion surrendered himself on March 12, denying that he had even gotten into the car with Duffy on Wabash. His story was backed up when state officials brought him into the cell where the witness who had fingered him was being held.

"If that's O'Banion, he ain't the fellow I thought he was," said the witness. "That ain't the guy."

What kinds of threats or bribes the witness had been given were not known, though everyone assumed something of that nature had taken place to get the man to change his story.

O'Banion was placed in protective custody in a hotel room, where he relaxed and chatted, claiming with a straight face that he "didn't mix with riffraff." Like Capone, he claimed to be a respectable businessman. "Why, I'm a florist. If I've ever been in the booze racket, I'm out now."

The whole affair helped build up Dean O'Banion's reputation in gangland. Everyone now knew for sure that he was able to take a man out, and able to make a man shut up, without facing any consequences other than having to spend a day or two in a hotel room. Obviously he was a dangerous man to trifle with.

But by meeting Duffy at the Four Deuces, O'Banion made a critical error. The meeting place had brought Capone and Torrio under suspicion, creating headaches for them. O'Banion created a lot of headaches for "the outfit" that Torrio had organized, and not all by accident. It's entirely possible that O'Banion had intended to make Torrio and Capone look like suspects by having the meeting in the levee. Simply running beer wasn't exciting enough for him, and he was always bugging Torrio to let him expand his territory. It probably would have been a relief for Torrio if Dean had been taken in by the cops for one of the murders and held in prison.

For the moment, though, they still needed O'Banion. There was a war brewing, and they needed everyone on their side they could get.

The Battle of Cicero

While the war between the Saltis-McErlane gang and the O'Donnells was racking up a body count throughout the city, Torrio expanded his empire, moving into suburban Cicero, an area that would soon become so thoroughly under gang control that people referred to it as "Caponeville." Here they could operate at least some of their organization away from Mayor Dever's meddling and his "war on beer."

Young Al Capone set up shop in Cicero, aided by his brothers, Ralph and Frank, who, like Al and John Torrio, were also veterans of New York's Five Points gang. Depending on whom you ask, Frank was either the businessman of the group or the most bloodthirsty of the lot, quick on the trigger and given to saying things like "I never got no backtalk from a corpse," while Al would have preferred to negotiate.

However, the notion that Al would have preferred to negotiate with anyone, especially at this point in his career, is almost laughable, and it was certainly Frank who represented the group in semirespectable dealings with the city of Cicero. City Manager Joseph Klenha and much of the town committee soon ended up on the gang's payroll.

The town of Cicero was run differently than some others—the government was set up by a "bipartisan agreement." Klenha was officially "president of the village board" but generally referred to as a mayor. However, when the spring elections in 1924 rolled around, the local Democratic Party put its own ticket on the ballot in a push to oust Klenha and rob the gangsters of their clout. Klenha and his men ran as Republicans (there had previously been no official party affiliations in city government in Cicero), and the gang decided to ensure its reelection, and its continued control of the area, with terrorism.

According to County Judge Edmund Jarecki, the election was "the worst in years." Rather than simply promoting their own "Republican" candidate, the gangs went after the opponents and their supporters with kidnapping, slugging, shooting, intimidation, and ballot stuffing. "General terrorism was the order of the day," the judge stated.

The night before the election, the office of William Pflaum, a Democratic candidate for clerk, was raided by members of Torrio's gangs, who shot the place full of bullet holes and beat up Pflaum.

On election day several Cicero precinct workers were kidnapped by the gangs and held prisoner in the basement of a plumbing supply shop. The police who raided the place found as many as twenty men blindfolded and bound to posts or anything else that was handy. Several bloodstains were in evidence. At least one Democratic worker was found tied up and blindfolded in the street; he had been held prisoner all through election day and then thrown out of a car when the polls closed. Another man was found at Cicero and Harrison hobbling helplessly on the ground and certainly unable to get to the polls, having been shot through both legs.

Those who made it to the polling place found trouble of their own. According to papers, "Many a voter was sent home with a broken head without having cast his ballot."

"Practically all the dirty work," said the judge, "was done by Chicago gangsters hired to go there and swing the election. The beer runners were all interested in the election, I am told, and Chicago's best gunmen were there to kill or terrorize whatever voters and workers were opposed to whichever candidates were friends of the gunmen."

Judge Jarecki begged Mayor Dever to send reinforcements into Cicero. Mayor Dever said he didn't have that authority outside the city limits but suggested that

Jarecki use his powers to deputize every last citizen in order to beef up his ranks. Jarecki brought a squad of Chicago cops into Cicero and deputized them as agents of the County Court—if the gangsters were bringing in Chicagoans, the government would too.

The cops were patrolling the area around 22nd and Cicero Avenue, nearby the Hawthorne Works of the Western Electric Company's factory and the Hawthorne Inn, the Torrio gang's main base of operations in the area. Just as many of the twenty thousand or so employees of the factory were pouring into the streets, ready to cast their ballots (or go drinking), the police recognized Frank Capone in the road along with two men, one of whom had a gun in both hands. They knew Frank by sight and assumed he was in town to cause trouble.

The cops armed themselves and jumped out of the car. Frank ran off, turning back occasionally to fire a gun of his own at the cops. Some witnesses later said he never fired his gun at all, but the cops said he fired twice before the third cartridge jammed his gun. But one of the bullets the cops fired pierced him in the heart; he fell to the ground, dead.

The man with a gun in each fist—a short, stocky man—began to fire at the cops before getting away. The third man was chased into a prairie and arrested.

The body of Frank Capone was taken to a coroner's office, where the man who had been arrested, Charles Frischetti, denied knowing who the mysterious third man was.

"Frank and I were thinking of opening a restaurant in Cicero," Frischetti said, by way of explaining why they'd been there in the first place. "We didn't even know there was an election being held out there."

Al and Ralph Capone were brought into the office to identify their brother's body, and a photo of Al talking with authorities became the first picture of him ever to hit the *Tribune*. Most stories told of the day years later claimed that Capone flew into a rage at his brother's death (some assume he was the short, stocky man with the guns who escaped), but newspaper photos show him looking calm and sad as he speaks with the officers about his brother's death.

In any case, the election ended the way the Capones had wanted it to: Klenha was reelected by a comfortable margin, and despite all the trouble, there was no call for a recount. But the victory certainly hadn't come without costs. The coroner's jury ruled the death of Frank Capone to be a justifiable homicide, marking the first major loss of life the Torrio-Capone group would suffer.

A Proper Send-off

Al and Ralph Capone threw their brother a lavish funeral in their home, the brick townhouse that still stands at 7244 South Prairie Avenue, where they lived with their mother. Three thousand flowers were purchased, and no one could take a step without walking on rose petals. Floral bouquets—six hundred of them—spread out of the house and onto the sidewalk outside, and $6,000 worth of flowers were still waiting in the shops to be delivered the next day. Ralph, Al, and their mother stood in the hall, receiving a stream of visitors that included Police Sergeant William Cusack and his squad—the very men who had shot Frank.

This was the first major gangland funeral of the era, and it would set the protocol for other gangland funerals over the next few years. Flowers came from every gang, including rivals like the Spike O'Donnell gang. A truce was called for the day, and all the gang's businesses in

Cicero were closed down for two hours out of respect. One hundred cars followed the hearse to the cemetery, including fifteen cars that were needed to carry the floral pieces.

The crowd was, to say the least, a curious mix. Gangsters stuck together, occasionally exchanging awkward glances with rivals who would normally have shot them on sight. Gunmen, beer runners, racketeers, and bootleggers walked alongside politicians and policemen.

Following a short service at the church, in which newspapers noted that many of the gangsters were attending their mother church for the first time in years and appeared nervous, the mourners proceeded to Mount Olivet cemetery, where the casket was lowered into the ground.

Even with all the paperwork and grave markings present, newspapers still referred to the dead man as "Frank Caponi."

And the truce certainly didn't last long: Frank's body was barely cold before the Torrio gang was double-crossed in a scheme that would set the great gang war into full swing.

With Friends Like These . . .

Besides the killing of Frank Capone, the Torrio syndicate's handling of the elections had one other consequence: It put them in a weaker position with O'Banion and his crew.

Torrio and the Capones knew it was better to have such a cast of characters working with them than against them and had always wanted to keep the peace with the O'Banion gang. Knowing that O'Banion was unhappy with his share of the city, and that they'd need more muscle to control the Cicero elections, they had asked O'Banion for help with their drive to ensure the victory of the side they favored. O'Banion had agreed to send two hundred men to Cicero on election day; in return, the Torrio gang promised to let him expand into Cicero, where he too could operate outside Mayor Dever's authority.

When the brutal election day was over, O'Banion was thrilled. Not only had he earned the right to expand his operations, but his day job as a florist allowed him to cash in nicely on the lavish funeral of Frank Capone. The new custom of gangsters buying tens of thousands of dollars' worth of bouquets when one of their own was killed certainly wasn't bad for business to this "man of flowers."

But O'Banion overplayed his hand a bit. He persuaded several Chicago saloon owners to relocate to Cicero (eager to get away from Mayor Dever's control, they were not hard to convince), and the booze he supplied to these new saloons was of higher quality than the stuff at the Torrio saloons. This raised competition for Torrio considerably. Torrio asked O'Banion to cut some of the other gangs in with a portion of his profits to make sure there was still plenty for everyone, but O'Banion declined. Any friendship that might have been growing between the two cooled off at once, with O'Banion livid that Torrio would even ask such a thing and Torrio livid that he'd refused.

Then, in an effort to keep life interesting (and raise profits), O'Banion hijacked a truck of booze that belonged to the Genna brothers, the Little Italy–based Sicilian gang that operated under Torrio's umbrella. This didn't make him any more popular with either Torrio or the Genna Brothers.

Only shortly thereafter, he would lead Torrio into a trap that would, in the end, seal his own fate.

CHAPTER SIX

Death of a Big Shot

The Gennas were six brothers—"Bloody Angelo," "Mike the Devil," Pete, Sam, Jim, and "Tony the Gentleman"—who had come to America from Sicily six years before. They were known as the Terrible Gennas, as their bloodthirstiness was basically unmatched by any other gang, up to and including the McErlanes. Tony was the exception. He was cultured and educated and didn't even live in Little Italy with his brothers; he preferred a $100-per-night suite at the Congress Hotel. He seldom got his own hands dirty; he *approved* of killings and presumably helped plan them, but he didn't get involved much himself in the actual operations. He felt that murder was beneath a gentleman like him. He was a dapper gangster—the kind who got a pedicure before going to the hospital for an operation.

Operating out of the Little Italy that had grown up around Taylor Street on the southwest side of Chicago, some miles from Little Hell, the Genna group had found a novel way to produce booze: They had a license to operate a brewery of their own (making nonalcoholic stuff, at least on the record) at 1022 West Taylor but had also found a notable loophole in the Prohibition laws: Rubbing alcohol was still legal to produce. They set up families—hundreds, by some estimates—all over their Little Italy stomping grounds around Halsted and Taylor with basement stills. The average home still could produce around 350 gallons per week, each of which cost about a dollar to make and sold for about six. The profits were huge.

But so were the expenses. There were some four hundred cops on the brothers' payroll, each taking bribes of anywhere from $10 to $150 a month for their services, both in looking the other way at the brewery and in busting private stills that operated outside the Genna operation. (Newspaper stories showing police busting a still was good for the Gennas' business, and they encouraged the cops to bust their rivals.) They also had to pay the families who ran stills in their houses, which wasn't cheap. All told, they were grossing hundreds of thousands every month, but after expenses they were left with about $150,000, to be split among six brothers. Twenty-five thousand dollars each per month was hardly chump change, particularly in 1923 money, but they always felt they could be making more. And with the sheer amount of booze they were producing, they had plenty leftover that could be sold in other territories. But moving to a new territory required the approval of Torrio —and would mean running afoul of whatever gang was running the territories they wanted.

But the fact that they might annoy Dean O'Banion was something that didn't bother the Gennas in the least.

While he was focused on Cicero operations in 1924, O'Banion seemed to let up his guard somewhat on his North Side home base, giving the Genna brothers, flush

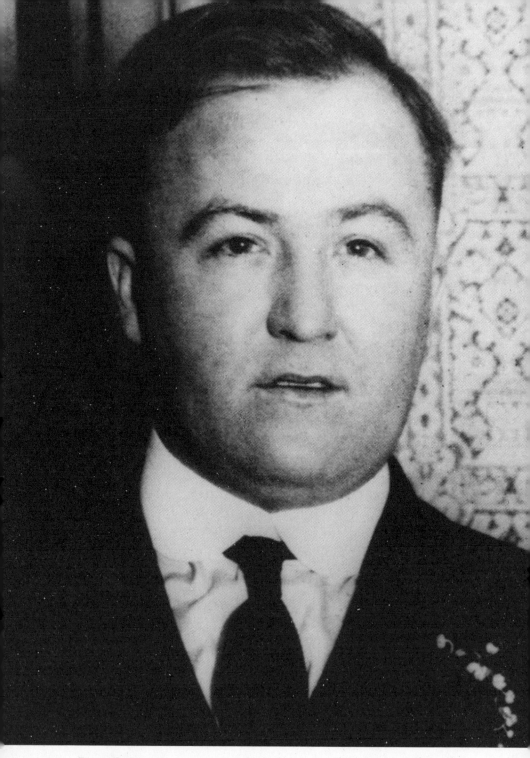

Dean O'Banion, who rose from being a singing waiter to head of the North Side mob PUBLIC RECORD

with rotgut liquor from home stills, a chance to start moving into the North Side and undercutting him on price. This was a violation of the treaty, but when O'Banion complained to Torrio, Torrio made no promises. He was still smarting from being brushed off by O'Banion in Cicero and perhaps wanted to pay him back by brushing *him* off in Chicago.

Furious, O'Banion ordered his men to fight back. They began hijacking the Genna brothers' trucks, including one shipment worth about $30,000. Behind the scenes, the Genna brothers held a family vote and unanimously agreed that O'Banion had to be killed.

But O'Banion was oblivious and kept to his old tricks. He didn't simply take his anger out on the Genna brothers, either—he determined to go after Torrio too. He was becoming convinced that Torrio, instead of being grateful for the help he'd given him in the Cicero elections, was planning to push him right out of business. Some say he believed the Genna brothers and the Torrio organization were part of an Italian conspiracy to keep Irishmen like him out of business.

So he set a trap for Torrio. In May 1924, only weeks after the tumultuous Cicero elections and the death of Frank Capone, one of O'Banion's police informants let him know that a raid was being planned on the Sieben Brewery, a plant just north of his native Little Hell that he and Torrio jointly owned.

A raid that found real liquor wouldn't do O'Banion much harm. He'd never been arrested for being in the beer business before, and he wasn't looking at anything more for his first offense than a fine he could easily afford. Given his classic luck, none of the other charges on him had stuck so far. He was still looking at trouble for being caught in the act of hijacking a truck back in January, but hijacking wasn't the same charge as brewing.

Torrio, though, had been fined once before, and another arrest with a prior conviction on his record would mean jail time.

Sensing a chance to humiliate his rival, O'Banion met up with Torrio and told him that he was sick of fighting, darkly hinting that he was sure that if he kept at it, the Genna brothers were sure to kill him sooner or later. O'Banion made Torrio one heck of an offer. He said he wanted out of bootlegging and offered to sell out his interest in the Sieben Brewery for half a million dollars—a bargain rate on such a profitable business. He even offered to help with one last shipment of beer that would be going out of the brewery on May 19.

The delighted Torrio suffered a rare lapse of good judgment and agreed to the deal, apparently not suspecting anything underhanded was going on. He arranged to meet with O'Banion at the brewery on May 19, just as O'Banion had suggested.

Thus O'Banion was able to ensure that the police would find Torrio at the brewery, and with actual beer—not "near beer"—in evidence. O'Banion knew he'd be arrested too but that he'd get off with a small fine. It would be well worth it to watch his rival's comeuppance firsthand.

So in the early morning hours of May 19, O'Banion and Torrio were both at the brewery, along with an armed convoy of several cars and trucks ready to transport the beer out of the brewery and out to the hiding places. But thirty police officers were lying in wait outside the building; they raided the place right around dawn.

Feigning shock, O'Banion ordered his men to surrender without a fight. Turning his charm up to full blast, he smiled at the police captain and said, "You ought to get a raise!"

Torrio was quiet, his face inscrutable.

Mayor Dever was over the moon about the raid, which resulted in more than thirty arrests (including two corrupt cops), the destruction of more than one hundred thousand gallons of beer, and a black book, believed to be O'Banion's payroll records, showing the names of several police officers who were working with the gangsters. It was perhaps the greatest victory his administration had scored over the bootleggers.

Of course, unbeknownst to the mayor, the whole thing had been set up by the head of the North Side gang to humiliate Torrio. With the information that the raid was coming, O'Banion could easily have made sure there was nothing incriminating inside the place on the day of the raid. At the very least, he could have arranged not to be there himself—and let Torrio know to make himself scarce as well.

But as O'Banion sat happily in his cell, waiting to be bailed out, Torrio must have looked on in disgust. He had no proof that O'Banion had set the whole thing up, and O'Banion wasn't about to admit it, but now Torrio was looking at actual jail time. This was trouble with the federal government—not the local cops that he could (and occasionally did) claim to own.

Furthermore, the brewery was now worthless, so the five-hundred-thousand-dollar investment he'd made in buying O'Banion's share was a total bust.

O'Banion didn't leave the city, or even appear to get out of the bootlegging game. He stayed around. But his luck was running out.

The Chicago Handshake

According to legend, the final straw for O'Banion came when word got back to Torrio that O'Banion had been overheard talking with Hymie Weiss and that Weiss had been pressuring him to make peace with Torrio before a gang war broke out. Supposedly O'Banion responded by saying "to hell with them Sicilians," which convinced Torrio that O'Banion had to go.

Although this story was current in Chicago by the end of the 1920s, it likely isn't true. Torrio himself wasn't Sicilian and surely had heard worse insults than that. Furthermore, there's not much reason to believe that Weiss would have pressured O'Banion not to double-cross Torrio. By all accounts, he had helped O'Banion set up the raid.

O'Banion got what he wanted—half a million bucks for a now-worthless brewery (far more than enough to cover any fines the arrest brought about) and a chance to send Torrio to jail.

But now he had both Torrio *and* the Genna brothers angry with him. He couldn't possibly hold out for long in a situation like that.

If he really *had* said "to hell with them Sicilians," it would have been an ironic statement: The only man keeping him alive at the time was Mike Merlo, head of the Unione Siciliana.

The Unione Siciliana was by then a nearly thirty-year-old fraternal organization working for the advancement of Sicilian-Americans. It provided insurance plans to Sicilians, helped them secure housing and jobs, and helped them to become Americans in general. It sponsored English-language classes, and while it celebrated many Italian holidays, it also threw massive celebrations on the Fourth of July and Memorial Day.

By providing these services, the organization helped ease the transition into a new country, providing familiar company and customs while introducing new ones. Its services were of untold value to recent immigrants trying to get on their feet. But critics noted that it was also keeping some of the old-world Sicilian customs, such as *omertà*, alive in the United States.

By 1924 the Unione was also phenomenally corrupt—and so connected to organized crime that later writers sometimes said Unione Siciliana was simply another name for the Mafia. Wielding its tremendous influence, the Unione is said to have bought and sold votes to the highest bidder. Even Torrio and Capone, who weren't Sicilian, were afraid to go against the Unione. Membership was in the tens of thousands, and control of the organization gave a man tremendous political power.

The Genna brothers, the only major gang largely comprising men from "that volcanic isle," as the *Tribune* put it, were high-ranking Unione members. The amount of money they were paying Sicilian families to put stills in their basement was significantly more than those families would have earned working in the stockyards, and many believed the organized criminals kept the unorganized criminals away. Anyone who tried to burglarize a house that was brewing alcohol for the Gennas, tried to crack the safe of a Sicilian-owned business, or was foolish enough to try any of the old Black Hand techniques would have been dealt with severely.

Mike Merlo, corrupt though he may have been, was genuinely concerned about the welfare of his countrymen. He was particularly opposed to murder. Assassinations, he believed, were bad for everyone—bad for business, bad for the neighborhoods. On more than one occasion, by most accounts, Torrio and the Gennas asked Merlo to authorize the killing of Dean O'Banion; each time he refused. As long as Mike Merlo drew breath, Dean O'Banion could not be touched without incurring the wrath of the Unione Siciliana.

However, there was a problem: Mike Merlo was dying of cancer.

Through the summer of 1924, O'Banion seemed to continue his lucky streak, swaggering through the city with a smile. Even in court he was confident and joking. In July he was brought to trial on charges related to January's botched hijacking. Newspapers by now seemed amused by the slippery gangster.

"Mr. Dean O'Banion," wrote Genevieve Forbes of the *Tribune,* "the modest north side florist whom the police are always surprising far from the gladiola beds and near the beer wagons, is resigned to a long absence from his American beauties . . . as he waits for the attorneys to select a jury to try him."

Indeed, jury selection wasn't easy. Finding jurors who couldn't be bought and who not only hadn't already made up their mind about O'Banion but also had no opinion regarding Prohibition was a long and arduous job. In New York, the Democratic National Convention was dragging into its second week as the disorganized party tried to agree on a nominee to run against President Coolidge. In Chicago, O'Banion "the genial purveyor of sweet peas," cracked that "it's gonna take them longer to get a jury than it'll take the Democrats to pick a candidate for President."

By the end of the first day, no jurors had been selected, and O'Banion was free to tell reporters "I'm not guilty. I want to run a florist shop if they'd only let me alone."

In the end, the trial was such a farce that a jury was barely necessary. The state had made a big deal out of their "star witness," Charles Levin. Levin had witnessed the whole hijacking. But on the stand Levin faltered. He told the court he was suffering from a lapse of memory and couldn't remember a thing about the night in question. The jury was unable to reach a verdict, and a mistrial was declared.

O'Banion's "immunity charm" was still working. He would have to go through the trial again eventually, but for now he was a free man.

In the end, though, the retrial would never take place—the defendant didn't survive long enough.

In early November a party was given for O'Banion at the Webster Hotel. Rumor has it that several policemen were in attendance and had helped with the grand presentation of a platinum watch to Dean. It would turn out to be a grim portent—the clock was ticking on O'Banion.

On November 9 Mike Merlo, the head of the Unione Siciliana whose word had kept O'Banion breathing, died in his home at 433 West Diversey. His death garnered only a small mention in the papers, but the Italians and Sicilians of the city came out in force to pay their respects.

Immediately, orders for flowers came in. A life-size image of Merlo created out of blue flowers—to match the color of the suits he often wore—was delivered to his house. Floral arrangements filled the house and spilled into the street; it was estimated that around $30,000 had been spent on floral designs and sprays alone. Hinky Dink Kenna and Mayor Dever were among those asked to be honorary pallbearers.

One order was called into Schofield's Flowers, O'Banion's shop, on the very night of Merlo's death. The man on the phone asked Dean if he'd be in around one o'clock. O'Banion cheerfully said that he would.

Apparently he had no idea that Merlo had been the man keeping him alive. And he certainly had no idea that the order had come from the Genna brothers.

In meetings shortly after Merlo's death, arrangements were made to put Angelo Genna in office as the new president of the Unione Siciliana. Far from there being a person to protect him, the office was now held by a man who wanted O'Banion dead more than anyone. Torrio wouldn't dream of holding the Genna brothers back from killing O'Banion, or anyone else they wanted to kill.

The Gennas by now had several hit men of their own in their ranks, including Samuzzo "Samoots" Amatuna, a personal bodyguard for Angelo Genna who was said to have killed plenty of men on the brothers' orders, and a pair named John Scalisi and Albert Anselmi, two thugs who had pioneered the idea of boiling bullets in onion juice and rubbing them with garlic so that a victim who didn't die of the gunshot might later die from gangrene. It seems these were the men the Genna brothers called to order the long-awaited hit on O'Banion. Crime writers would come to know Scalise and Anselmi as the "Murder Twins."

The next afternoon O'Banion worked at his flower shop, perhaps glancing out the window at the cathedral where he had sung in the choir as a young boy. A young boy, Gregory Summers, was helping younger kids from the parochial school cross the street in the early afternoon. Mr. Schofield was out at the cemetery, fixing up graves for Armistice Day.

William Crutchfield, a shop employee, was sweeping up the floor when three men walked into the store— "short, stocky and rather rough-looking."

When O'Banion came out from the back, he seemed genial with the man, indicating that he knew them, or at least had been expecting them.

"Hello, boys!" he said. "You from Mike Merlo's?"

"Yeah," said one of the men.

Crutchfield, not liking the looks of the men, headed for the back room as the tallest of the men shook O'Banion's hand vigorously. He was safely in the back when he heard the first five shots. There was a brief pause before he heard the sixth.

All six shots were hits. Two were in O'Banion's chest, two were in his throat, and one was in each cheek. The delayed sixth shot seemed to have been done at even closer range; there were powder burns all around it.

Crutchfield came back out just in time to see the men leaving. The boy who had been helping younger kids cross the street told police that he saw three men run out—two of them "were dark and looked like foreigners," while the other had a "light complexion." They had jumped into an automobile and driven off west before he could get a better look.

William Schofield came back and answered questions as the body was taken away. He continued taking calls, saying, "You want a floral wreath? I'm sorry but we can't take your order. We've had an . . . an . . . an accident here. And I guess we'll want all our floral wreaths at that."

A reporter grabbed a phone in the shop and put in a call to Mrs. O'Banion, identifying himself as a reporter.

"Oh, my God," she screamed at once. "It's Dean, I know. What has happened to him? Is he dead?"

In the aftermath, the police called in everyone—Al Capone, John Torrio, the three Millers from the fracas at the La Salle Theatre (all now fully recovered), Hymie Weiss, Vinnie Drucci, and others. They were all questioned and released.

Chief of Detectives William Shoemaker was cynical in his questioning of Weiss. "If you knew anything about this murder, would you tell me?" he asked.

"Well, to be frank, I guess I wouldn't," said Weiss.

More Funerals

It was to be a week of funerals in gangland. First there was Merlo's, which was attended by a crowd estimated at ten thousand. He was buried at Mount Carmel Cemetery.

O'Banion owned a large burial plot in the same burial ground. The church put up a fight against having such a gangster interred there, but as he had been convicted of no murders and hadn't been a suicide, they couldn't deny him burial (though they did deny him Christian rites).

The lack of a blessing didn't stop the funeral from being one of the most massive the city had ever seen, putting even Frank Capone's to shame. The body laid in state for three days in the Sbarbaro funeral parlor at 708 North Wells, where the undertaker did a fine job removing the powder stains from the cheeks so that the corpse would look presentable.

In fact, the body was beyond simply "presentable." The casket was an elaborate one—reporters variously gave its value as between $7,500 and $10,000. It had been brought in from the East in a special train car that carried no other cargo, and according to reports it was made of solid silver and bronze walls, with a white satin "couch." There were solid silver posts carved in "wonderful designs." It must have seemed a shame to bury such a fine piece of work right away.

Mrs. O'Banion sat sadly at the head of the casket, lighted by the countless candles that lined the place and surrounded, of course, by flowers. Lots and lots and lots of flowers. Al Capone sent a basket of roses. The International Brotherhood of Teamsters sent a wreath. In all, it was said that there were *twenty-six truckloads* of flowers.

Everyone came out for the funeral, where Weiss, O'Banion's most obvious successor, was said to be seen crying "as women might." The sidewalks were jammed elbow to elbow with the gangsters, the mourners, and the curious for blocks running north and south of the funeral home, and hundreds more people stood on the roofs of the building. There was a six-piece orchestra in the funeral parade. At Mount Carmel, it was said that five thousand people had already gathered before the body was even put into the hearse.

For all this, though, there were no photographs allowed—gangsters were vigilant about this. Cameras were snatched from photographers. Many of the gangsters were ready to use force against the reporters—or one another—if need be. No one expected any flare-ups at a funeral, but one had to be prepared in case of emergencies, so most of them came fully armed and ready.

Many reformers were appalled at the affair. What child of the poor neighborhoods could see the display and *not* think there was nothing so grand as the life—or death—of a gangster?

But the funeral and burial ended no differently than the burial of a poor man in the potter's field at Dunning Cemetery—with the dead man buried beneath the earth to rot away.

"Now O'Banion is dead," wrote the *Tribune,* "others [are] marked, and the police [are] wondering where the next bullets will be turned loose."

Only weeks after O'Banion's death, a rumor flew through the underworld that "Scarface Al Brown"—Capone—had been shot to death. Police spent the better part of the morning chasing the rumor before finding Capone, alive and well, at his home. With a grin, he paraphrased Mark Twain in telling the police that reports of his death were "greatly exaggerated."

CHAPTER SEVEN

Revenge Follows Revenge

Then came a war.

Any observer could see that a war was already going on in the city, but before the murder of Dean O'Banion, the heads of the gangs seemed safe. The killings were mostly the result of reckless men storming around the city with firearms, money, booze, and a belief that they were above the law—a dangerous combination to be sure. But these killings were really just random flare-ups. Accidents, really. Merlo's influence had kept a lot of men safe from one another.

Torrio was probably the most measured and rational of all the gangsters in town, in addition to being the most powerful, but even he wasn't above the law. He knew full well that allowing the murder of O'Banion wouldn't exactly endear him to the North Siders. He made an appearance at O'Banion's funeral—a bold move if there ever was one—then immediately got out of town to lay low over the holidays. He reportedly traveled to Hot Springs, Arkansas, from there to Havana, Cuba, and from there to Florida. He returned to Chicago in early January 1925, and it was said that he had been followed all throughout the South by "several of O'Banion's most loyal followers."

If Torrio thought things had cooled down with the weather, he would soon find that he was badly mistaken.

Just a day or two after Torrio returned, a car owned by Ralph Capone, Al's surviving brother, was shot up at 55th and State. Thirty shots were fired into the car as it moved down the road, driven by Sylvester Barton. One of the bullets managed to sear Barton's flesh, having cut right through his clothes. Two other people in the car—a couple of waiters who had just waited on the gang at a restaurant—were unharmed.

Police believed that Al Capone—who the papers now called Scarface Tony or Al Brown—was the real target of the attack, though he hadn't been in the car at the time. No one thought it was a serious assassination attempt. No hired gangland killers could possibly have missed thirty times unless they intended to. These were only warning shots fired across the bow, a signal that a real fight was coming.

A couple of days after the shooting on State Street came the trial for the Sieben Brewery affair. O'Banion was to have been on trial along with Torrio, but, as the judge noted, he had already been dealt with. This was a federal case, and Torrio's influence and pull didn't extend beyond the state and local levels. He was sentenced to pay a five-thousand-dollar fine and spend nine months in the DuPage County jail. O'Banion's plan to double-cross Torrio was continuing to work from beyond the grave.

"These are the types of men who put the courts to shame," Judge Cliffe barked. "We might as well close the courts as let them go unpunished. Dean O'Banion and John Torrio were the chief conspirators in this case, but O'Banion [was] murdered in cold blood by criminals of [his] own class since the indictment, and no further attention need be paid [him] by enforcement officers."

District Attorney Olson was harsh, both with Torrio and with the local officials who had failed to put him behind bars years ago. "These are outlaw gunmen," he sneered, "who ought to have been prosecuted by state authorities years ago for robbery, murder, or other crimes. But they were allowed to pursue their criminal careers. It remained for the federal government to give them their first experience behind prison bars, and that had to be done on a common liquor charge!"

Torrio was given ten days to arrange his affairs before going to prison.

A week afterwards, during his brief window of freedom, Torrio came within a hair's breadth of not being able to serve a day.

No single person had stepped into O'Banion's place as head of the North Side gang. Hymie Weiss, Vinnie "The Schemer" Drucci, and "Bugs" Moran jointly took over and began serving as a sort of "board of governors" overseeing the "business" along with Louie "Two Gun" Alterie and "Dapper Dan" McCarthy. Alterie was quickly asked to leave town and was smart enough to do it (his loudmouth persona and tendency to challenge people to shoot-outs raised Weiss's ire), but the remaining four spent the early winter of 1924 making plans to avenge their fallen leader.

On January 24 Torrio, enjoying his last few days of freedom before his jail term, took a limousine to the Loop to go shopping with his wife. When they returned home to their remarkably modest home on South Clyde Avenue, Torrio gathered packages from the seat and took his time getting out of the car.

Across the street sat a gray car containing Moran, Drucci, and Weiss.

Two of the men came out of the car as Torrio fumbled with the packages, splitting up to approach him from opposite sides, and opened fire.

Everything happened quickly—as a few neighbors and even a few cops looked on, gunshots pierced the winter air. In a burning instant, the driver of Torrio's limousine was shot in the knee as one man shot a .45 caliber pistol into the windshield while the other man fired buckshot into the rear of the car from a sawed-off shotgun.

Torrio managed to get out of the limousine unhurt and ran toward his house, but as he raced for the door, a shot from a revolver caught him in the arm; he reeled around in shock and pain. As he did, a fresh load of buckshot caught him just below the face, breaking his jaw and cutting holes into his lungs and side. He fell to the ground.

According to legend, the man with the revolver, Moran, approached the fallen gangster and held the pistol to his head, telling him to "say good-bye" and preparing to give him a coup-de-grace shot in the face to finish the job, echoing the final shot given to O'Banion. But when he pulled the trigger, nothing happened; he was out of bullets. He didn't have time to reload before a third man in the vehicle—either Weiss or Drucci—honked the horn and gave the signal to flee. Newspaper reports from the time didn't quote Moran as actually saying anything pithy as he knelt to finish Torrio off, but the rest of the story about him failing to kill Torrio because he ran out of bullets seems to have been correct. If there had been a bullet in the gun, Torrio would have been nothing but a stain on his porch.

Mrs. Torrio, showing remarkable composure considering the situation, dragged her wounded husband into the vestibule of the apartment, where she tried to stop the blood that was pouring out of his jaw and neck. A passing police officer hauled Torrio into a cab, which took him to the hospital; Torrio barked orders to cauterize the wound before he bled to death as they rode along.

Torrio's chauffeur, Mr. Barton, had sped away in the limousine as soon as Torrio was out of the car. A nearby police officer saw the car speeding by with bullet holes in the windshield and gave chase, eventually overtaking Barton at 71st Street. Loyal to the code, Barton refused to say what had happened, even though Torrio wasn't his actual boss. The car belonged to Jack Guzik, whose brother Torrio had just arranged to keep out of jail. Guzik had left for New Orleans, leaving the car and driver with Torrio as a way of saying thanks. Under the circumstances, few would blame Barton for telling whatever he knew—getting shot at was surely above his pay grade. But he knew the code and followed it.

Once in the hospital, it was apparent that Torrio was going to live. But true to the *omertà*-like code that had been adopted by all the gangs, he refused to talk. "Yes, I know them," he said, "but I won't tell."

Later reports claimed he said, "It's my business."

Even Mrs. Torrio refused to name names. "What good would it do?" she asked. If she had ever truly believed that her husband was simply a businessman, as many of his friends later claimed, those days appear to have been over. She didn't seem incredulous that someone would try to kill her innocent husband.

Al Capone, visibly shaken, was taken into custody for questioning. In his shocked state, he nearly forgot the code. As he waited outside Torrio's room, he repeatedly said, "The gang did! The gang did it!" But he got control of himself and declined to elaborate.

The police were frustrated, but they expected no other reply from Torrio's friends and family and seemed to have no hope that the assassins would be brought to justice. Captain Steige told reporters that they might be able to figure out who did it with a pencil and paper "but never with a judge and jury."

However, the police had a pretty good idea that the O'Banion gang was involved and specifically named Drucci, Moran, and Weiss as suspects along with Frank Gusenberg, a hit man who was rising through the ranks of the gang. None could be found for questioning.

Torrio survived and was placed under heavy guard at the hospital to prevent someone from finishing the job. He declined to press charges, and no one—not even Moran, who was identified in a lineup by a brave teenage witness—was ever indicted.

Another Gang Loses a Leader

Immediately upon his release from the hospital, Torrio was taken to prison. There, with his considerable funds, he was able to arrange for a private, roomy cell with a comfortable brass bed, an elaborate Oriental rug, and a nice desk. Three deputy sheriffs were hired as guards. A bulletproof screen was erected over the barred window, and dark curtains were hung so that no would-be assassin would be able to see his shadow as he paced about the room, listening to the opera records he was allowed to bring in.

While in prison he made perhaps the best decision any Chicago gangster ever made: He decided to get out of the business. While he was incarcerated, he told a visiting Al Capone that he was going to retire and that control of the entire outfit would go to him.

Things seem to have gotten off to a fairly rocky start. While Torrio was in prison, the organization he had built nearly went up in flames—literally. The outfit had set up an office for "Dr. A. Brown, MD" at 2146 South Michigan, where behind the fake waiting room was a clerical office run by Jake "Greasy Thumb" Guzik. Here they kept track of paperwork, including names of hotels and other buyers; income from their booze, gambling, and prostitution rings; records on bribes; and other incriminating evidence. All of this had previously been done at the Four Deuces, but once the resort became too well known, the more secretive aspects of the operations were taken to the new office.

In early April 1925, as Torrio sat in his cell, detectives burst into the offices, stunning the half dozen or so employees, one of whom offered Sgt. Edward Birmingham $5,000 if he left the bookkeeping system alone.

In the section of the office that looked like a waiting room, half-pint bottles of booze were lined up in an "orderly array" to be sampled by the "patients."

By all rights, this raid should have been a major coup. The detectives were in possession of the names of more than two hundred patrons of the outfit, the names of the officers on the Torrio-Capone payoff list, the routes along which booze was imported from Canada and the Caribbean, and all the data they could need to shut down countless breweries, brothels, and saloons in Chicago and the suburbs. A telephone bill for $287 showed that the operation was a busy one.

However, the raiders had made one fatal error: They had failed to get a warrant to raid the office, meaning the investigation had been an unconstitutional case of search and seizure. On April 10 Judge Howard Hayes ordered the records to be returned to "the syndicate" before they could be inspected by the government. Mayor Dever, who had triumphantly crowed "We've got the goods now," was once again left with his tail between his legs.

In the midst of the controversy, the very day the judge ordered the records returned, Capone was arrested. Police pulled him over for speeding and arrested him for having revolvers in his car; he was booked at the station, where his attempts to make bond failed. Unlike his previous displays, though, Capone simply smiled, relaxed, and ordered $25 worth of steaks for himself and his fellow prisoners. It was stories like this that began to popularize a new nickname for Capone: "Big-Hearted Al." He certainly liked this name better than "Scarface," and at times it seemed as though he was trying to live up to it.

Capone was freed the next day, and with the trouble from the raid behind them, it was already apparent that the organization was in good hands.

Upon Torrio's release, several armed cars escorted him to the East Coast, where he and his wife boarded a ship for Italy. But Italy was under the leadership of Benito Mussolini, whose fascist party did not look kindly on countrymen who had left for the United States, and Torrio didn't remain in Italy long before returning home. He settled in New York, far from the guns of Chicago, and O'Banion's men seemed content to let him go. After all, they knew he wasn't the one running things anymore. Killing him wouldn't have changed the business at all. Capone was the next obvious target, and with Torrio gone and O'Banion dead, many people believed that Capone was next to be killed.

The North Siders, though, had set their sights on another gang first. They knew the Gennas had taken O'Banion down, and now the Gennas had to go.

CHAPTER EIGHT

The Brief Reign of the Genna Brothers

With Torrio gone and O'Banion dead, whatever alliances the gangs of the city had honored before crumbled. Old partnerships shattered. Allegiances shifted. Territorial lines were ignored.

Though the North Siders hated Torrio and Capone, they never believed they were the ones who had personally pulled the trigger on O'Banion. They seem to have figured out right away that it was the Genna brothers' doing, and as Weiss, Moran, and Drucci got their gang reorganized, the Genna brothers became their primary targets.

Angelo Genna had ascended to the presidency of the Unione Siciliana, and the power seemed to go to his head. Forget Capone—he was now, at least as far as *he* was concerned, the most powerful man in Chicago. Even Capone, who was still technically his boss in the outfit, wouldn't have dared to go against him and risked upsetting the Unione.

Flush with cash and power, Angelo had recently married Lucille Spignola, daughter of a prominent

Sicilian man. At their January 10 wedding, there were around three thousand guests and a wedding cake newspapers remembered months later as the largest ever seen in the city, weighing in at around two thousand pounds.

In June 1925, as the dust from the "doctor's office" raid was settling, Angelo was driving out to Oak Park, in the first layer of suburbs outside the Chicago city limits, to pay for the handsome new house he'd bought for himself and Lucille. He was heading west on Ogden when a sedan carrying four men pulled up along beside him. According to the lone witness, the sedan appeared to chase the Gennas' roadster for a minute before a man leaned out the window and fired a dozen shots, several of which hit Angelo. Losing control, he crashed the automobile into a light post.

The four men drove away, leaving Angelo to die.

He was still alive, but not expected to survive, when he was brought into the Evangelical Deaconess Hospital, where he followed *omertà* and refused to talk.

Detective Sergeant Roy Hessler leaned over and gave it to Genna straight. "You're going to die, Angelo," he said. "Tell us who bumped you off."

But the dying man simply shrugged his shoulders.

His devastated bride had no luck getting him to talk. She knew nothing, she said, about the rumors that Angelo had just won something like $35,000 rolling dice on the South Side. Or about the black book full of nicknames, telephone numbers, and notes about barrels of alcohol. She didn't even know that he had been on his way to pay $11,000 for a new house; they had been living in a $400-a-month suite at the Belmont Hotel. As was the custom for recent gang widows, she said she certainly didn't know that her husband was a bootlegger, or that any gang might have suspected he'd had a role in the murder of Dean O'Banion, or about any power struggles within the Sicilian community.

By the end of the day, Angelo Genna's body was in an undertaking parlor on Taylor Street.

Lucille and her brothers-in-law all insisted that Angelo had no enemies and that everyone had liked him. And during his typically lavish funeral three days later, it seemed that had been true. The Genna brothers purchased Angelo a $6,000 casket—bronze and silver, just like O'Banion's, and so heavy it nearly broke the back porch when it was taken out of the house to the hearse. The body was dressed in rich purple robes to hide the dozen or so unsightly bullet holes that marred it. As usual, the funeral became a morning-long truce as members of rival gangs arrived in peace, all with lavish floral displays in tow. All the people who had hated Angelo in life sang his praises in soft voices now that he was dead and gone.

The Gennas of course had a motive behind the lavish displays—the funeral *had* to be better than O'Banion's. And everyone knew that was their plan. Seventy-five thousand dollars worth of flowers filled the three-story townhouse of Angelo's father-in-law, Joseph Spignola, where the bier was kept—many purchased from Schofield's Flowers. Even John Torrio was able to send a huge vase full of carnations from prison. Capone sent lilies.

"The interment, some six months ago, of Dean O'Banion, that other outlaw of the Volstead game, who played and won and played and lost, was the yardstick by which they measured Gennas' ceremonies of yesterday," wrote *Tribune* reporter Genevieve Forbes Herrick. It was generally estimated that O'Banion had drawn a larger crowd, but onlookers noted that with O'Banion, the mob was largely curiosity seekers. The crowd here was all *friends*.

A procession of thirty-one limousines—a cortege a mile and a half long—took Angelo Genna's remains to

Mount Carmel Cemetery, where he was laid to rest only a stone's throw from the resting place of O'Banion himself. Mike Merlo was nearby as well.

Forbes Herrick credited one man at the graveside with the most memorable line of the day: "There's Mike and Dean and (Angelo) Genna. When judgment day comes and them three graves are open, there'll be hell to pay in this cemetery."

The unnamed man had no idea how right he was. There would be far more gangsters in Mount Carmel by the end of the gang war. Eventually even Capone himself would be rotting away beneath the soil there, alongside several other gangsters who were set to fall along the way. Today the cemetery is a veritable Who's Who of mobster graves

And there was still a war to fight. The identity of the men in the car who shot Angelo was never determined, but police had a few logical suspects: Bugs Moran, Vinnie "The Schemer" Drucci, Frank Gusenberg, and other North Side mobsters with a clear motive to get rid of the Gennas. The fast-and-furious style of the drive-by shooting had all the hallmarks of a North Sider job. Few people in the know doubted that the North Siders had declared war on the Genna brothers to avenge the death of Dean O'Banion.

In any case, the Gennas were all marked men. Just two weeks after Angelo Genna was buried, his brother Mike "The Devil" became the second Genna brother to be struck down in one of the more spectacular chases of the gang war.

Mike the Devil

By June 13, 1925, the war was in full swing. That morning, Bugs Moran and Vinnie "The Schemer" Drucci got into a minor scuffle with Mike "The Devil" Genna and his two top assassins, John Scalise and Albert Anselmi, the two men generally thought to have pulled the trigger on O'Banion, when they ran into one another on the West Side. In the dust-up Drucci was wounded in the leg, just the first casualty of a day that was to be full of them.

According to a later report, by that time it wasn't just the North Siders who wanted the Gennas eliminated. The South Siders, now led by Capone, are said to have wanted the Gennas out of the way as well. Their hold over the Unione Siciliana was a roadblock to Capone, who wanted someone more loyal to him leading the organization. (Since he was Italian not Sicilian, he couldn't have the job himself.) The fact that the Gennas' own determination to kill O'Banion had brought about the attack on Capone's mentor shouldn't be overlooked either. The Gennas may have been at the height of their power, but they had more deadly enemies than anyone else in town.

Scalise and Anselmi were loyal to Capone first and foremost, and according to later reports, the two were actually taking Mike for a ride with the intention of killing him when they ran into Moran and Drucci, who were *also* waiting around to kill Mike.

If that was the case, it was clearly Mike's time to go that day. He would be attacked by the North Siders, his own men, and the police in three separate scuffles that day—a day when it seemed as though everyone was secretly plotting to kill everyone else.

That June morning, Mike Genna was out with Scalise and Anselmi, alias the Murder Twins, and Sam "Samoots" Amatuna, one of the Gennas' confederates, all of whom may have been planning to kill him. Scalise and Anselmi might have been secretly taking Mike for a ride, and the North Siders had apparently offered a huge reward to Samoots if he could arrange for them to kill Mike by delivering him to the corner of Sangamon and Congress, where they could shoot him from a nearby car (as was their usual method of execution). But while Samoots wasn't necessarily aligned with the Gennas, he sure wasn't on the North Siders' team either. After pretending to accept the offer, he told the Gennas of the plan, and a counter-plan was hatched. This, so far as we can tell, was the real mission of the day: to go to Sangamon and Congress to kill Moran and Drucci. But if that was the sole purpose of the mission, it's hard to imagine why Mike himself had to be there at all. Why didn't he just send Scalise and Anselmi?

On the morning of June 13, the four men went to the corner, fully armed. Moran and Drucci sat together in a parked car, presumably waiting for Genna to come as Samoots had arranged. But then the Genna-Scalise-Anselmi-Amatuna car snuck up behind them and fired buckshot into their car. Moran and Drucci managed to fire a few shots of their own and chased the Samoots' car for a block or two, but the bullet-ridden car couldn't go far.

Whether Scalise and Anselmi were really taking Genna for a ride at the time, not just ambushing the North Siders, can only be guessed at now. A later "confession" by another gangster said it was all a big setup and that Capone had hoped to end the day with Moran, Drucci, and Mike Genna all dead. In any case, Samoots drove the car away from the scene with all the major players in the drama still alive, although Drucci was wounded.

But the day wasn't over. As Samoots steered the car down Western Avenue, it passed a police car containing police officers Walsh, Conway, Olson, and Sweeney.

"There's a bunch of hoodlums," said one of the cops.

Officer Conway spied Mike Genna specifically among the crowd and suspected they were on their way to a liquor pickup. "We'll follow them and see what they're up to," he said.

They pulled up in pursuit with a siren blaring, and the gangsters in the car took off. Soon a full-fledged car chase was under way. The police car got up to seventy-three miles per hour heading south down Western by the time a truck swerved in front of the gangster's car. Samoots, at the wheel, swerved and slammed on the brakes. His vehicle spun around, jumped a curb, and crashed into a lamppost.

The cops slammed on their own brakes and came out to confront the four men—peacefully.

"What's the big idea?" asked one, as two of the men emerged from the car. "Why all the speed when we were ringing the gong [siren]?"

Rather than a verbal response, gunfire exploded from the back of the gangster's car—Scalise firing a repeating shotgun from the back seat. Officer Olson fell to the ground, his jaw torn neatly away from his face. Another volley of bullets caught Officer Walsh in the chest.

Officers Sweeney and Conway pulled out their own guns and began to fire.

In the firefight Conway fell quickly as bullets sprayed his own chest; he fell to the ground. Sweeney continued to fire as the gunmen began to run from the car—Scalise and Anselmi ran into a garage, still carrying their guns, with Mike Genna following close behind. As they ducked into an alley, Genna turned back and fired a shotgun at Officer Sweeney—or tried to. The gun, out of ammunition, failed to go off. Sweeney fired himself, hitting Genna in the leg.

Several off-duty cops had by then joined the chase. While Genna busted a basement window and ducked inside to hide, two new cops on the scene busted through the cellar door. They found Genna, lying weak and bleeding from a ruptured artery in his leg. They carried him out, calling for an ambulance.

In the midst of the firefight, Samoots Amatuna had made a clean escape. Scalise and Anselmi ran into a store at 59th and Rockwell, where they tried to buy a couple of hats to disguise themselves. When the store owner refused to sell them any, they left to run toward Western Avenue, where police saw the exhausted (and still hatless) men boarding a street car. The officers chased the car down and began exchanging blows with the men. The Murder Twins were apparently not as good with their fists as they were with firearms; the fight ended with the two men under arrest.

Walsh and Olson, two of the fallen police officers, were rushed to the German Deaconess Hospital, where both men soon died. Officer Conway was still in critical condition at the end of the night.

For his part, Mike Genna still had one good leg, and as the officers put him on the stretcher to be taken to a hospital himself, he used it to kick one of the officers in the face. "Take that, you son of a bitch!" he shouted.

But that kick took whatever energy he had left; he died from blood loss only minutes later.

When the news of the fight reached City Hall, Mayor Dever met with Chief Collins and began to seriously discuss a plan of arming police squads and sending them out to shoot gangsters on sight. They eventually decided to wait on that plan, at least until the next police officer was killed. Cops would be cracking down harder on the gangsters from now on, but "armed squads" wouldn't be released just yet.

Still, Collins's men wanted revenge on the gangsters for the shooting of their brothers in arms, and

Detective Shoemaker was himself out for blood. "We have reached a time," he said, "when a policeman had better throw a couple of bullets into a man first and ask questions afterward. It's war. And in wartime you shoot first and talk second."

Scalise and Anselmi, who had quite possibly been planning to kill everyone with whom they came into contact that day, sat in a prison cell as State's Attorney Robert Crowe told them he knew they'd killed Dean O'Banion, and that he was going to see to it that the two of them hanged for the murder of the police officers.

In response the two men simply claimed they'd never seen each other before in their lives; they'd just been out looking for work when they were arrested. The fact that multiple witnesses identified them didn't faze them a bit.

Capone meanwhile put wheels of his own in motion. He raised money (sometimes at gunpoint) to give Scalise and Anselmi a $100,000 defense fund and began machinations to get Tony Lombardo, one of his men, established as head of the Unione Siciliana. Capone, being Neapolitan, couldn't even join the Unione, but he longed to control it and its wide political powers.

But he had to deal with the cops first. On June 14 more than fifty raids were undertaken, largely in the home stills the Genna brothers had set up. In the raids, 320 suspects were arrested. Ten thousand barrels of mash and ten thousand barrels of alcohol were seized, along with many weapons. Newspapers showed the police proudly standing on the barrels and showed crowds of Italian immigrants who had been arrested as suspected gangsters and bootleggers. Among the places raided was the Gennas' stronghold at 1022 West Taylor. There the police found six leather-bound record books that laid bare the whole of the Genna brothers' operations. Every name, every address, and every price was in the books, right down to the gas bills (which for some cookers reached $100 a month). There were even names of doctors who could be trusted to keep quiet if they were called on to treat a man who had been shot by the cops or other gangsters.

As police crowed about the discoveries, they dealt the Gennas another blow: Mike Genna's funeral would not be a flashy one. The body was kept in seclusion, and the police announced that any and all mourners at the gravesite would be taken in for questioning. The burial was done very quietly, with none of the lavish displays that had become the norm for gangsters, while the fallen police officers were buried as heroes.

And the Genna brothers' bad summer wasn't even over yet.

Tony the Gentleman

On the morning of July 8, 1925, Tony "The Gentleman" Genna received a call at his residence, supposedly from one Giuseppe Nerone, a man known as *Il Cavaliere*. Nerone was a part of the Genna gang but was said to be annoyed that the Genna brothers had failed to appreciate him as much as he thought they should. Tony still trusted him (or whoever it was on the phone), though, and arranged to meet him at Cutilla's grocery store at Grand and Aberdeen.

Whoever met Tony at that store was waiting with two "torpedoes," a gangland term for a sharpshooter, hiding around the side of the building. The man took Tony's hand and said, "Mister Genna, my fren'," and the two torpedoes ran up behind Tony and fired three shots into him. Charles Cutilla Sanphilippi, the grocer, thought he was being robbed and shouted "Don't shoot me; I'll pay!"

As Tony was raced to Cook County Hospital, suspicion immediately fell on Moran and Drucci—police had only recently learned about the dust-up between those two and Mike Genna on the morning of Genna's death. When Assistant State's Attorney John Sbarbaro came into Tony's room at the hospital, Tony smiled at him and said hello.

"Who shot you?" Sbarbaro asked.

Tony began with reluctance, and perhaps a lie. "The gang," he said. "Americans. I'd tell you if I knew, but I don't."

But Genna's brother Sam begged him to give more information.

"Tell the police," he begged. "It's the only hope for me and my kids. Otherwise they'll kill us too."

Tony considered this as he lay dying. Perhaps he and his brothers had felt that Mike's death, even so soon after Angelo's, was just a fluke. But this sealed it—the Genna brothers were clearly marked for death. Tony opened his mouth and with what little breath he had left said, "Cavalerro," a presumed reference to Giuseppe "Il Cavaliere" Nerone.

Nerone wouldn't live long, but his death the next year came at the hands of a whole other gang, not the Gennas, who were now living in terror. Of the three surviving brothers, Jim was said to be in Europe, Peter was in hiding, and Sam was begging for a police escort to follow him around wherever he went. By 1926, when Nerone was killed, the Gennas were in no position to kill a man at all.

Tony wouldn't get a big funeral either. The day after his death, he wasn't even in a coffin but lying on a slab in a funeral home with a small crucifix on his breast and small candles at his head and feet. Only a few curious passers-by came to look. He was given a simple funeral at the De Cola Funeral Home on Grand Avenue, barely a block away from the grocery store where he met his fate.

The tomb of the Genna brothers, within sight of Capone's grave
PHOTO BY AUTHOR

Sam and Peter Genna attended, but practically no one else did.

Though the police continued to suspect the remnants of the O'Banion gang of Tony's murder, the brothers told them otherwise. Since their home stills had given them such a huge supply of booze, they had been undercutting

Interior of the Genna brothers' tomb at Mount Carmel PHOTO BY AUTHOR

other alcohol dealers, and that had made them a lot of enemies in the area.

Many suspected a Unione Siciliana power struggle, but former judge Bernard Barasa denied that the brothers were even members, or that the organization had any connection to organized crime. "The Gennas," he said, "would have been killed if they were Irish, Polish, German, Americans—anything. They were killed because they were bootleggers, and they were killed by other bootleggers."

With Tony interred at Mount Carmel near Mike Genna, Dean O'Banion, and Mike Merlo, Sam and Pete fled. Their empire was over.

But the era of gang funerals was not.

Samoots

There is still some debate as to whether Mike Genna was already being "taken for a ride" by Scalise and Anselmi when the police killed him (on the same day that Moran and Drucci tried to kill him). It seems incredible to imagine that the guy would have two gangs out to kill him on the very same day, even more incredible that he was killed by someone else that same day. What a coincidence that would be!

But one critical piece of the puzzle suggests that Genna was being double-crossed by the men in the car: If the driver was in fact Sam "Samoots" Amatuna, Mike's bodyguard, then it's fairly telling that the bodyguard ran away at the first sign of trouble with the cops.

Then again, being a bodyguard doesn't seem to have been the kind of career Samoots had in mind for himself. He had lots of other things on his plate at the time.

Samoots was known as something of a "Beau Brummel" in the bootlegging world. Like Tony Genna or John Torrio, he was enamored of the arts, but he showed more personal flair than either of them. In 1921 his personal worth was said to go "from nothing to thousands" overnight, and he spent $40,000 in cash to buy himself a restaurant.

Rather than buying a brothel like everyone else, he purchased a jazz cabaret called the Bluebird Cafe at Halsted and Taylor Streets. He had so many friends among the patrons that he boasted he was safe enough not to need to carry his guns in the cafe. Occasionally he would take the stage himself to sing in his pleasing tenor voice. Surviving photographs make him look far more dashing than most of the other gangsters of the era. With his cut jaw and stylish hat, he could have gone on to be a star in the era when Hollywood was seeking real gangsters to star in gang movies.

But Hollywood would have to settle for second-stringers like Spike O'Donnell, because men like Samoots wouldn't live that long.

Sam Amatuna first became a significant presence in the newspapers in 1921, when he was arrested in his cafe to the strains of the jazz band for the murder of Paul Labriola, whom he and Angelo Genna had killed as part of a political power struggle between Angelo d'Andrea (who would soon be killed himself) and others for control of the 19th Ward and of the Unione Siciliana. Labriola had been shot and killed in broad daylight outside a building at Halsted and Congress, only blocks away from the Bluebird. Less than a week later, the police determined from eyewitness accounts that Samoots was the killer and had him arrested.

But the police wouldn't give the names of the witnesses. "I received my information from a source which I would never reveal," said Sergeant Alcock of the police. "The man's life would not be worth a cent if I told. As it is . . . I am sure I have the right man."

The police raged about how bad Little Italy had gotten in those early Prohibition days. The neighborhood around Halsted and Taylor had never been that great to begin with. Hull House, the settlement house where Jane Addams practically invented American social work, stood right in the middle of it, as it had since 1856, when Charles J. Hull built his family mansion on Halsted. In those days it was practically the prairie. By the time Addams moved to town in 1889, the mansion was sticking out like a sore thumb in a slum neighborhood to rival the Five Points. Even Addams's pioneering work hadn't exactly made the neighborhood desirable by the 1920s. Samoots would have had to run right past Hull House (by then a thirteen-building complex) to get back to the Bluebird after killing Labriola.

Alderman Powers, whose own rivals and supporters were on opposite sides of the bloody struggle, decried the area himself. "We have not only political hatred and killing to fight in my ward," he said. "There are numberless hangouts for criminals, all sorts of desperate characters, that have been thriving for years. . . . Among these dives are a number of rotten poolrooms, where gambling has been consistent and open. Here there congregate crowds of youthful desperadoes who, when they have no money, will not work, but they will go out and kill somebody to get money."

But as convinced as the police may have been that Samoots had killed Labriola, the case lacked admissible evidence. He went free, going on to rise in power.

In the summer of 1925, the year the Gennas were slaughtered, he made a number of enemies himself.

Though Capone had tried to install Tony Lombardo, one of his own men, as head of the Unione Siciliana after Angelo Genna's death, he was thwarted when Samoots walked into the organization's headquarters and announced that *he* was the new head. The Unione backed him up as the new leader, shutting Lombardo (and Capone) out.

This made Samoots a marked man, both by the North Siders and by Al Capone. Not to mention that he always had the threat of jail over his head. Police figured out early on that he was probably the missing fourth man in the car when Mike Genna was killed but never had enough evidence to hold him.

He lasted until November 1925, when he was shot on the first anniversary of the murder of Dean O'Banion (an anniversary that escaped no one in Little Italy).

Samoots had been consolidating his power and enjoying his new status. He bought a new set of tailor-made suits, a diamond pin, a diamond watch chain, and a diamond ring. Though he had risen to considerable prominence in the old Genna empire—the stills he now controlled in their absence generated plenty of cash for one man—he had begun to talk about settling down. He got engaged to Rose Pecaroro, the sister of Mike Merlo's widow. At twenty-six years old, he was ready to retire.

A week before the wedding, he planned to take Rose to the Auditorium Theatre to see *Aida* and went to a barbershop at Halsted and Roosevelt to get himself done up properly for a night at the opera. As he stood up from the chair, neatly groomed and newly shaved, his nails newly polished by the shop's manicurist, two armed men walked into the barbershop and began to shoot. They fired eight times, then jumped into a getaway car and escaped.

Samoots's friends quickly converged around his bleeding but still-living form, and he ordered them to take him to his cigar shop on Taylor, around the corner from the Bluebird. Soon he was taken from there to the Jefferson Park Hospital, where it became known that if Samoots survived, he would likely be paralyzed for life.

That it was the anniversary of O'Banion's death escaped no one, but as Samoots Amatuna lay in his hospital bed, theories as to who had shot him and why flew through the city like snowflakes in a streetlight. Some said it was revenge for a hijacking job he'd pulled a couple of weeks before. A few said it could have been the work of angry loan sharks—Samoots had appeared flush, but one friend said he was $22,000 in the hole. When the police had knocked over all those Genna stills, Samoots had claimed that more than half of them were actually his, not the Genna brothers'.

Others said that someone else simply wanted him out of the way in order to take control of the Genna brothers' stills. And some speculated that someone wanted to make sure his wedding to Rose Pecaroro never took place, as it would have brought with it considerable status and power in the Sicilian community, cementing Samoots's status as head of the Unione.

Naturally Samoots himself wasn't talking, even though he was still capable of talking for a time. He may have known the identity of the shooters, but he wouldn't say anything in the hospital, other than to occasionally ask for a glass of water, while his brother Luigi, newly brought to the United States and unable to speak English well, sat in the hall, struggling to comprehend what was going on. "Say only that he will live," he said to the doctor, "and you can have $50,000; $100,000. Anything."

Rose, Samoots's fiancée, cried at his side as he slowly slipped away. He was only able to talk a little, but he and Rose decided that if doctors determined that he wasn't going to make it, they would bring a priest in to marry them right there in the hospital before he died.

For more than a day, Samoots hung in the balance between life and death. Preparations for a deathbed wedding were made, but Samoots fell unconscious before it could happen. He died late at night the day after his shooting, with only two doctors and a nurse at his side, still unmarried.

Police continued to warn that there were to be no more elaborate gangland displays for the funeral, but now the Sicilian community and the underworld seemed inclined to ignore such rulings; Samoots was buried in style. Word went out among his friends that "Samoots will have one of the biggest funerals ever held in Chicago."

Even with all his enemies, people apparently liked Samoots, just as they had O'Banion. He was a swashbuckling dandy who boasted that he never carried a gun. He spent money freely and was happy to let Angelo Genna take credit for many deeds of charity that were really his own. "Sure," one of his friends told a reporter, "if he wanted a guy knocked off, he'd have him knocked off, what the hell? But he was a good guy just the same."

So they sent him out in style. A wake was held at Rose's house, and the funeral was at the De Cola's Funeral Home on Grand Avenue, near the site where Tony had been shot and in the same place where Tony's body had been on display. But this was not to be anything like the small party converging around a body on a slab that had been Tony's funeral; Samoots was placed in a $10,000 casket of the now-customary silver and bronze and surrounded by $20,000 worth of flowers (from Schofield's of course). The flowers filled Rose's house, along with the backyard, the front yard, and then the front yards of several neighbors on Seminary Street. Sam Amatuna was eventually buried at Mount Carmel but would be exempt from any battles that occurred on the promised day when the bodies rose up from the graves, as his remains were later exhumed and transported to a burial place in Sicily.

The list of suspects for the killing was a long one, but two men who would have normally been prime suspects weren't on it: Scalise and Anselmi were still in custody, having been sentenced to fourteen years in prison for the murder of the two police officers in the shootout that killed Mike Genna. Even this sentence was a victory for them—and a hard-fought one. One major witness had his house bombed. But a gangland lawyer convinced the jury that it was really a case of manslaughter, not murder, saving the men from the gallows.

They wouldn't be in prison nearly that long of course. Through Capone's considerable influence, another jury would eventually conclude that the two men had only reacted to unnecessary police aggression; they would be free to walk the streets again.

They were still in holding, though, in November when Samoots was killed, making them about the only two killers who *weren't* suspects in his shooting.

Some now claim the killers were two men from the North Side gang, most likely including Frank Gusenberg, who were either trying to get revenge on everyone connected to the Gennas for the O'Banion killing or taking revenge for the fact that Samoots hadn't followed through on a deal with Moran to kill Mike Genna himself on the day when Genna may have been "taken for a ride." However, eyewitnesses described the killers as "dark" men who looked Italian or Sicilian. A more common theory today is that Capone sent his men to get Samoots out of the way so that he could install someone else as president of the Unione Siciliana.

In any case, for such a popular man, Samoots had a lot of enemies in town.

And with him out of the way, there was nothing stopping Al Capone from moving forward with his own plans. Tony Lombardo finally became head of the Unione Siciliana and immediately opened up membership to people of other nationalities, making Capone a member at last.

CHAPTER NINE

Capone's First Mistake

Throughout 1926 Al Capone began to become famous outside Chicago. When he took over the leadership of the gang, he brought to it a sense of PR that other gangsters had lacked. As he became more and more of a media figure, the people of Chicago almost seemed to take pride in their city's budding reputation as the criminal capital of the world. When people who had moved to Chicago took trips back to their hometowns, they were expected to have a few gruesome stories about men in pinstriped suits shooting guns out of car windows into crowded streets.

After all, the public at large didn't feel they were living under any threat of violence personally. Now and then someone might get caught in the crossfire, but though there were dozens, even hundreds, of murders a year in those early days of the "beer wars," it was really all just the bootleggers shooting at one another. People who just wanted a drink now and then had nothing to fear.

Capone in the early 1930s, toward the end of his reign
PUBLIC RECORD

Indeed, rarely has a whole nation been so proud to flout a law. The people running stills for the Genna brothers made several times more money than they would have made in a factory. And even if they *were* feeding into a system that was built on crime and killings, what other choice did they have, really? Was working at the factories any better? Didn't lots of factories make a whole pile of money building supplies from the recent Great War in Europe? That had killed a whole lot more men than the gangsters ever could.

At the center of the whole system stood Al Capone. There was something about Capone that simply fascinated people. Just months after he took over for Torrio, stories of his power and influence spread far and wide, and many people truly admired him.

But things took a turn for the worse in 1926 with the shocking killing of William McSwiggin, a twenty-six-year-old prosecutor in the office of State's Attorney Robert Crowe.

With so many gangsters getting away with murder under Crowe's watch, people were beginning to whisper that Crowe must be on the take, and the city's anti-gangster element set its hopes on Billy McSwiggin, a rising star who had pulled off convictions in nine capital cases in a row (though none of them involved gangsters). Known as Little Mac to his friends, and as "The Hanging Prosecutor" to others, McSwiggin was a smart, sharp-witted young go-getter who dressed just as well as the gangsters did and seemed like he could be the one to outsmart them and bust up the gangs.

But he had grown up in tough Irish neighborhoods playing stickball with the same guys who were now running bootleg liquor around town on the North Side, and he was known to remain friendly with some members of the Klondike O'Donnell gang who were now operating on the West Side (not to be confused with the South Side O'Donnells run by Spike and his brothers).

By the spring of 1926, the Klondike O'Donnell gang was one of the last organizations on the West Side to be battling the Capone gang. Capone's penchant for opening brothels was said to be offensive to the somewhat more religious O'Donnell gang, who saw young Al as a degenerate. But Capone saw these O'Donnells as little more than an annoyance as he pushed them slowly out of Cicero. The two groups had been allies once, at least on paper, but those days appeared to be over within a year after Torrio left town. Capone slowly chipped away at the Klondike O'Donnells, hoping eventually to take over all their territory.

On April 27, 1926, William McSwiggin was standing with two other men in front of the Pony Inn, a saloon at 5613 West Roosevelt in Cicero. The other two men were James Doherty and Thomas Duffy, who made up much of the upper command of what remained of the Klondike O'Donnell gang. Inside the saloon were Miles and Klondike O'Donnell themselves.

A scout in Capone's organization saw Klondike's prized Lincoln automobile sitting out in front of the saloon and immediately informed Capone that a few of his rivals were only about a mile away from the Hawthorne Hotel. Capone gave the impulsive order to pull the trigger and take them out.

As McSwiggin and the two gangsters stood in the parking lot, a car with curtained windows pulled up on the road and leveled the barrel of a Thompson submachine gun through the curtains. When it came close enough, a flurry of gunfire shot forth from the barrel. Some of it hit the Lincoln automobile; some of it hit the men.

All three men were killed; Doherty and McSwiggin probably died instantly. Their bodies were quickly loaded into a car by the O'Donnells and disposed of on a prairie road. Duffy was brought to a hospital, where he joined the other two in death hours later.

When the bodies were found the next morning, the city was shocked—what had McSwiggin, the hanging prosecutor himself and the last best hope of the local gangbusters, been doing in the company of a couple of gangsters?

As soon as news of the shooting came through, Robert E. Crowe rushed out of bed, where he had been when he heard the news, and assembled his entire company of detectives. He barked out orders that every single questionable character—the usual suspects—were to be rounded up at once. "Every beer runner, every gunman, every bootlegger, and every other kind of racketeer in the reach of an officer of the law," he roared.

The first place newspapers listed as having been raided the next day was "The Hawthorn hotel in Cicero, the hangout of Al Brown, the Italian leader of the Cicero gunmen." Even as Capone's fame spread, papers continued to call him Al Brown or Al Caponi for years, depending on what he was calling himself at the time.

As the raids continued, theories about what the heck McSwiggin had been doing in the company of such men flew. The *Tribune* identified three possible motives for his slaying:

1. Revenge for his having prosecuted John Scalise and Albert Anselmi. He and Crowe had both received death threats, and McSwiggin had just told a reporter that he'd turned down a $30,000 bribe from the gangsters to help free Scalise and Anselmi. Papers splashed a photo of McSwiggin, looking like a younger Clarence Darrow, arguing for the hanging of the two men. (He eventually failed; no gangster of the Prohibition era was ever hanged.) This theory

may have been correct, but it didn't explain what he was doing in the company of gangsters.

2. Crowe suggested that McSwiggin had been in Cicero to gather evidence undercover, and gangsters had killed him upon finding out who he was.

3. McSwiggin was an old friend of Duffy and of Doherty and was still on friendly terms with them, though not in league with them, even though he had prosecuted both of them for killing a Cicero resort keeper two years before. He had just been catching up with old pals from the neighborhood, not up to anything unsavory, and happened to get caught in the crossfire.

Crowe roundly ignored the theories that McSwiggin had been friendly with any gangster and stuck to his theory that Little Mac had died a martyr's death. Soon his investigation was focused on Al Capone. "It has been established," he stated, "that Al Capone in person led the slayers of McSwiggin . . . five automobiles, carrying nearly thirty gangsters, all armed with weapons ranging from pistols to machine guns, were used . . . it has been found that Capone handled the machine gun."

This was probably a wild exaggeration. Capone was very unlikely to be pulling triggers for himself at this point in his career, now that he was in a position to have jobs like that done for him.

However, he was concerned enough to duck away to Michigan for a few months to wait until the whole thing cooled off. He was arrested briefly but released due to a lack of evidence.

"I'll tell you what I know about the case," Capone told reporters. "I had nothing to do with the killing of my friend, McSwiggin. Just ten days before he was killed, I talked with McSwiggin. There were friends of mine with me. If we had wanted to kill him, we could have done it then and nobody would have known. But we didn't want to . . . I liked the kid. Only the day before he was killed, he was up at my place, and when he went home, I gave him a bottle of Scotch for his old man."

This was just the kind of chatter that made Al Capone famous. People loved to believe he was really a good man at heart, friends not just with the cops but also with the man who'd tried to have two of his own men hanged. He made it look as though any trouble they had from the cops was nothing personal. But this time Capone's charm wasn't swaying everybody. McSwiggin's old man was a sergeant in the police force. If he ever got the Scotch, it didn't matter. As the summer of 1926 wound to a close, he told authorities he believed Al Capone had killed his son.

Every authority seems to have believed Capone was responsible, but there was simply no evidence to prove it. Most likely Capone wasn't lying when he said he didn't want to kill McSwiggin; McSwiggin had probably just been a bystander who was caught in the crossfire when Capone ordered the hit on the men from the O'Donnell gang.

But this time it was no ordinary bystander; it was a state's attorney. And his killing led to two major ramifications.

For one, news that McSwiggin had clearly been friendly with gangsters—the O'Donnells for sure, and maybe even Capone himself—was a jolt to the law-and-order wing of the city. Their golden boy, it seemed, had just been another two-faced flunky who was friendly with the mobsters he was supposed to be prosecuting. Faith in the local authorities waned even more.

But even more important in the long run was the result of one of the many raids carried out: While authorities were raiding Capone's Hawthorne Hotel, they confiscated a bookkeeping ledger. The ledger was brought to a police station and put into an office closet by authorities who seemed not to know what they had. There it would begin to gather dust. Years later, though, it would be instrumental in Capone's downfall—tangible proof that Capone had been earning an income in 1926, which meant he should have filed an income tax return.

But that downfall was still a few years away, and during those years, Capone would become the most famous gangster in the world.

Shooting Up Cicero

Meanwhile, the North Siders decided to make a stand of their own.

On September 20, 1926, a parade of eight automobiles rolled into Cicero. Each of the cars carried three men with machine guns. Passengers are thought to have included Earl "Hymie" Weiss, Vinnie "The Schemer" Drucci, George "Bugs" Moran, Frank "Tight Lips" Gusenberg, and all the other major players from the North Side mob. Though gang leaders and other higher-ups usually used hit men to do the jobs, this particular parade was so fully armed by so many men that the principals of the North Side mob almost *had* to have been there. Drucci in particular was hungry for blood, as an attempt had been made on his life only days before.

That attempt had been something for the locals to talk about. Drucci and Weiss had been about to enter the new Standard Oil building on South Michigan Avenue when several men from the Capone gang emerged from a car with guns blazing. Drucci and Weiss ducked into a parked car, pulled guns of their own from shoulder holsters, and shot back. One bystander was hit, and countless others ducked for cover. It was rush hour on Michigan Avenue, so thousands of people on their way to work got to watch the drama unfold.

Ever a crazy and reckless man, Drucci jumped from the vehicle and started charging right at his attackers, who fled from the spot. When taken in by police, Drucci denied that the Battle of Standard Oil had been a gang fight at all, insisting that it was just a battle with a "couple of punks" who were trying to rob him.

He and Weiss were shot at again only days later in almost exactly the same place. By then they knew exactly who was responsible: The Standard Oil Building was at Michigan and Ninth, only a short walk from the Metropole Hotel, which Al Capone was now starting to make his home base.

Now, weeks after the Battle of Standard Oil, as the caravan of North Siders rolled into Cicero, the men with machine guns—twenty-four in all—leaned out the windows and unleashed a barrage of bullets from their weapons as they cruised slowly past Capone's Hawthorne Hotel. An estimated thousand bullets were fired into the building.

There were surprisingly few casualties—the worst damage came to a bartender who was hit in the shoulder.

Al Capone had just left the building but knew as well as anyone that he had been the primary target of the massive, frontier-style assault. In the year or so since Torrio had left town, Capone had become the undisputed king of the city. How much money he was making is impossible to determine, but estimates for his gang's earnings in 1926 vary between $30 million and $100 million.

Capone was the king now—the man to cut down.

Much is made of the contrast between Torrio and Capone. Torrio never carried a gun and traveled without a bodyguard, while Capone was endlessly paranoid. But in hindsight, Capone was being smarter. Torrio was shot and nearly killed right in front of his own house. After that no one in his right mind who was in control of a large gang would go out in public without adequate protection.

And Capone was the king now—the meatiest target in town for more enemies than he could count.

The New King

When he rose to the top of the gang, Al Capone was only twenty-six years old, though he looked at least a decade older. He was rolling in money; though he officially owned no buildings other than his house on Prairie, he was known to "control" several of them. He held no bank account and worked in cash, wearing pants that were specially tailored to have extra-deep pockets that held rolls of bills in high denominations— mostly $100s and $500s.

In a recently released 1931 letter from the archives of the Internal Revenue Service, an agent wrote that "Alphonse Capone is, without a doubt, the best advertised and most talked-of gangster in the United States today." The letter described him as a "punk hoodlum" who had come to Chicago around 1920 as a protégé of Torrio and had emerged in the 1926 newspapers as "Capone, the immune, Capone, the idol of the hoodlum element, Capone, the dictator, free from arrest and persecution by the local police due, no doubt, to his lavish spending of money and giving bribes."

Capone was not as quiet, confident, or assured as Torrio had been. He was always armed, and he never traveled alone. Bodyguards were with him at all times.

If the stories of Capone's niece Deirdre are to be believed, Al Capone was endlessly paranoid and had nightmares about being shot at, one of which involved having several cars forming a line of machine gunmen shooting at him. When the dream nearly came true with the assault on Cicero, he began to dream up ways of getting out of the business. According to Deirdre, Capone floated ideas of starting a fashion line, buying the Edgewater Beach Hotel, or purchasing the Chicago Cubs. Wrigley Field, he said, was his favorite ballpark, and buying the park on the North Side would have been an interesting symbolic move for him.*

But Capone stuck with the outfit, and rather than crawling into a shell of security, he took the then-unprecedented step of becoming concerned with PR. Gangsters had seldom courted the press before.

"The first time I ever saw the man," Tony Berardi, a photographer for the *Chicago Evening American* recalled, "was at a police station. . . . At the beginning he used to cover his face with his hands, a newspaper, whatever. He never posed for pictures at that point. More than once or twice I saw him try to beat up photographers."

According to Berardi, it was his boss at the *American,* Harry Read, who talked Capone into changing his ways when he became the big shot chief of the city. "He said, 'Al, look, you're a prominent figure now. Why act like a hoodlum? Quit hiding. Be nice to people.'"

Capone took the advice to heart. He became known for giving out horse race tips to strangers (if Al Capone told you a horse was going to win, it was a sure bet), giving large tips to waiters, and shaking every hand he could reach. He gave his friends lavish gifts, such as jewel-encrusted belt buckles. (Harry Read got a jewel-encrusted watch.)

Berardi didn't like Capone personally and insisted that most other people didn't either. "There were roughly five hundred thousand Italians in the Cook County area,"

....

* It should be noted that Deirdre, daughter of Capone's brother Ralph, was only about six when Capone died.

he said, "and out of that entire group maybe five hundred admired Al Capone. Italians were and are honest, hardworking people, and they had no respect for him. . . . [But as] much as I didn't like the guy, I have to admit he was good with kids. He sure helped a lot of people that I heard about when they were in arrears with their rent. He was a charitable guy." Still, Berardi believed that he damaged the reputations of Italians throughout the city. "Christ," he recalled, "if your name ended with an *e, i,* or *o,* everyone thought you were a member of Capone's mob or one of his relatives."

Capone, a sports fanatic, began to attend lots of sporting events, including regular boxing matches on Thursday night and several baseball games. Giving out racing tips was a way to hand out bribes without *actually* handing out bribes, making it good for business as well as being good for public relations. Simply telling reporters or police officers to bet on number 6, a horse running at 60-to-1 odds, wasn't actually the same as giving them money, even if it did put a lot of money into their pockets, and reporters weren't likely to be too hard on people who helped them make money.

Capone (at least according to rumor) made friends with the *Tribune* as well. Colonel McCormick, then publisher of the venerable newspaper, brought Capone to the paper's headquarters and asked him to help prevent a strike that the drivers' union had been threatening. Capone saw to it that there was no strike.

This may have never happened. It may just have been a story that William Hale "Big Bill" Thompson concocted to smear the *Tribune,* whose management hated his guts, when he ran for mayor again. But it helped create the sort of image Capone wanted to cultivate—a man of the people, ever willing to lend a helping hand and use his money, power, and notoriety to help people.

Capone became a regular fixture at City Hall, glad-handing and making all the friends he could as he presented himself to the public as a crafty, well-dressed man with nothing to hide and nothing to fear.

Much of the public bought the act completely. To them Al Capone was a source of fascination—a self-made man if there ever was one. Many believed he never actually killed anyone himself; that gangsters only killed one another, never any innocent bystanders; and that Capone was at heart simply a normal man who had done well for himself—a regular guy who just happened to control wide swaths of the city. When a reporter went to his Prairie Avenue house, he found Capone wearing a pink apron and cooking up a pot of spaghetti, a look Capone probably carefully planned.

Soon Capone was in control of most of the South and West Sides. The gang moved out of the seedy Four Deuces and into the Metropole Hotel at 2300 South Michigan. Police claimed they'd successfully pushed the gang out of Cicero, but Capone smiled and scoffed, explaining that he simply needed a bigger place. "My interests have expanded," he explained, "and I required a central headquarters."

The Metropole Hotel was not nearly as opulent as Capone's later headquarters at the nearby Lexington Hotel. It was a seven-story dive perilously close to City Hall, where Mayor Dever continued to fight against Capone. The hotel, wrote Jonathan Eig, "tended to attract traveling shoe salesmen and farmers making the infrequent drive to the big city to trade their old vehicles for new ones. . . . It was the sort of place where retired men in casual clothes would sit in the lobby chewing toothpicks."

One particularly notable feature of the Metropole was that it was connected through a series of tunnels to other nearby hotels. The tunnels had been built years before as a means of transporting mail, coal, and garbage in the colder months, but they served another handy function: In the event of another raid, or another assault from the North Siders, the gang could make an easy escape.

Now Capone had a kingdom to protect, and after the assault on the Hawthorne, as Capone worked on moving his headquarters and building up his "nice guy" image, he gave the order that Hymie Weiss, the closest thing the North Siders now had as a leader, had to go.

CHAPTER TEN

The Bark of the Guns

As Capone grew throughout 1926 from being a "punk hoodlum" to a central figure in American mythology, it was said that he feared no man except Earl "Hymie" Weiss, who by then was generally spoken of as head of the North Side mob. No one spoke of a "board of governors" running that operation anymore. Papers simply referred to "the Weiss Gang" when they spoke about the haze of machine-gun fire that had been pumped into Capone's buildings in Cicero.

Capone of course had hit men of his own to exact his revenge.

Jack McGurn, later known as "Machine Gun" McGurn, had risen through the ranks to become as close a confidant as Capone had. Still in his early twenties, McGurn had come to the United States in 1906 at the age of three under his birth name of James Vincenzo Gibaldi. He took on the more "American-sounding" name of McGurn as a teenager as he pursued a career in boxing.

McGurn didn't grow up surrounded by crime and vice, as many of the other mobsters had. His father owned a cafe and seems to have operated on the level. But in January 1923, as Jack and his young wife were preparing to have their first child, his father, Angelo, was receiving threats from one of the last groups of Black Handers who hadn't yet been pushed out of the city. One day that month Angelo was tending to a customer, holding three buffalo nickels the man had just used to pay him, when several Black Handers said to be affiliated with the Genna brothers came into the cafe. One fired a shotgun into Angelo's chest, sending him flying backwards. A second bullet blew his face to smithereens before his body even hit the ground.

Jack arrived on the scene minutes later and, according to legend, soaked his hands in his slain father's blood, took the buffalo nickels from the ground, and made a solemn vow of revenge. The damage to his father's face ensured that the funeral would be a closed-casket affair—a particular insult in the Sicilian community, where tradition held that the casket should be left open for two days and nights to allow the soul to ascend to Heaven. During the funeral, a friend of Angelo who had been in the cafe at the time of the murder is said to have slipped Jack a piece of paper containing three names: the names of his father's killers.

Jack continued his career as a boxer but began to spend his spare time perfecting his marksmanship by shooting birds off telephone wires around the streets of Little Italy, using the only gun he owned at the time—a Daisy repeating rifle BB gun he bought at a sporting goods store for ten bucks. It was the easiest gun for a beginner, but it was still hard to practice his marksmanship without arousing suspicion in the neighborhood. He supposedly took to practicing during neighborhood celebrations so that the gun fire would blend in with the sounds of the firecrackers.

He became remarkably proficient in a very short time, and by the end of March, he felt he was ready to take his revenge. He arranged to take ten days off from work and purchased a proper pistol. With it he methodically killed each man whose name had been on the piece of paper he'd been handed at the funeral.

Like most gang stories, the story of McGurn's revenge and his rise to prominence as a hit man is probably a mix of fact and fiction, but certainly *something* caused him to attract the attention of the gangsters. He found himself getting part-time work for the Circus Gang, a small gang working for Capone under the direction of Claude "Screwy" Maddox. Soon he had attracted the eye of Al Capone himself and began doing small jobs for him personally. When his boxing career fizzled out, McGurn became a full-time gangster with Capone. He began to emulate him, dressing in snappy suits and spending money lavishly.

Though he reported to the Capone gang in Cicero, McGurn continued to live in the heart of Genna territory, where his stepfather was working in distribution. (Some later said he was the Gennas' principal alcohol cooker, though this was probably nonsense.)

Throughout 1926, as Capone began to level vengeance against the North Siders for the killings of the Genna brothers the year before, as well as the attacks on Torrio, McGurn became Capone's top hit man and a favorite in the organization. Some say it was he who told Capone that Hymie Weiss had to go.

The Death of Hymie Weiss

Walk down State Street today and there's a parking lot where Schofield's Flowers, O'Banion's old shop, used to stand.

Across the street is the Holy Name Cathedral. Local legend has long held that the small hole in the cornerstone is a bullet hole from a gangland killing long ago. Some sources say it's actually a hole from a plaque that used to be on the cornerstone (shots from Tommy guns don't leave such neat little holes), but it's certainly in just the right place for a bullet hole to be, and there *were* gangland bullets fired there once. In fact, the cornerstone was badly damaged during the assassination of Hymie Weiss in October 1926.

By that time, the North Side mob was dealing with the trial of Joe Saltis, of the Saltis-McErlane gang. Though they came from the South Side, the Saltis-McErlane gang had somehow managed to remain largely independent of Capone and had formed an alliance with Weiss. Now Saltis was on trial for murder, and Weiss had raised about $100,000 for his defense.

Frank McErlane too was in trouble. He had been arrested for the murder of Thaddeus Fancher, an attorney from Crown Point, Indiana, and in July 1926 he was facing extradition to Indiana to stand trial. In a scene that embarrassed the hell out Chicago's more honest authorities, when he was brought into the courtroom, McErlane and his guard were both visibly drunk and reeking of whiskey. Clearly gangsters had no trouble getting booze, even when they were locked up, and the guards weren't doing much to stop it.

The judge noted McErlane's condition, then looked to the guard. "I guess an expert is not needed to determine that he too is drunk," said the judge.

The guard was immediately suspended and taken away. As they dragged him to the back room to relieve him of his badge, the drunken guard got angry. "Let me get back at that judge!" he shouted. "And I will knock him loose from his trousers!"

Another prison guard was also clearly drunk and was suspended as well. Both guards denied having given any booze to McErlane, but *someone* obviously had.

"This is a serious situation," the judge noted. "If men in jail can obtain liquor, they can obtain guns."

Frank McErlane was acquitted a year later. The case against him seemed solid at first, but after the main witness against him was hacked to death with an ax by "person unknown," there was no one left to testify.

Meanwhile, Hymie Weiss spent the summer of 1926 consolidating power on the North Side, in the process becoming an ever-more-irritating thorn in Capone's side. Had he been nothing *more* than a thorn in Capone's side, things might have gone back to Torrio's old "plenty for everyone" ethos. But Capone knew that if Weiss got Saltis out of a murder rap and formed a solid alliance with him, it could mean a lot more trouble. It might even have led to McErlane wanting to shoot him. No one would have wanted a psychopath like McErlane gunning for him.

Hymie's personal fortune was fairly small by gang standards; estimates a couple years later put his worth at $1.3 million, give or take half a million bucks. Members of the gang, in their usual way, described him as a pious man who was always fingering a rosary (gangsters are almost always described as devoutly religious by their friends). When people weren't calling him pious though, they generally referred to him as mean, crude, and violent. He would threaten to kill anyone who took a picture of him, and one photographer said he had a "face like a savage."

Savage he was, but perhaps Hymie really did finger a rosary constantly, always trying to make himself right with God, always fearful that the end could soon come for him just as it had for O'Banion. There was talk that he had premonitions of his own death; a gangster in his position would probably have been foolish *not* to have such premonitions. One day one of his drivers complained of the hard work he put in for fairly paltry pay—he had seen firsthand just how much money was rolling in. "Jeez," he said to Hymie. "I'd like a cut with you. It's coming awfully easy for you."

Hymie appeared morose as he looked at the driver and said, "I'll trade places with you."

According to legend, this meeting took place in October 1926.

Two days later Hymie was gunned down across the street from Schofield's Flowers, in front of Holy Name Cathedral, in a barrage of machine-gun fire that blew a few words off an inscription on the cornerstone. EVERY KNEE SHOULD BOW IN HEAVEN AND EARTH became EVERY KNEE SHOULD . . . HEAVEN AND EARTH. The cornerstone was not repaired for years.

Capone had made one last shot at peace. According to stories told later, earlier in October Capone had attempted to set up a peace conference. While he didn't attend himself, he sent Tony Lombardo, the man he'd installed as head of the Unione Siciliana, to meet with Weiss and said he'd do "anything within reason" for peace. Weiss's demand is said to have been one that Capone had to refuse: that Jack McGurn be turned over to the North Siders to be taken for a ride.

Two days after the peace overtures, a man who called himself Oscar Lundin checked into a rooming house at 740 North State Street, right next door to Schofield's Flowers. The second-floor room with a view was unavailable, so Lundin moved into a hallway room and bided his time, moving into the room he wanted when it came available.

This gave Lundin (who was presumably McGurn) a view of the sidewalk outside Schofield's Flowers, which continued to be a hangout for the North Side mob. They would often congregate right in the spot where their original leader's blood had flowed from his lifeless body.

While Lundin set up camp, hiding out and meeting with visitors to the rooming house whom witnesses described as "swarthy" and "Sicilian," Weiss busied himself trying to rig the jury for the Saltis trial. He became a regular fixture in the courtroom, which was only a short walk from Schofield's, and carried with him a list of the names of men on the jury. In the safe at Schofield's, he had a list of names of men who would be called to testify against Saltis.

By October 11 Lundin and another man in a boardinghouse a few doors down had been staking out the area around State and Superior for a good week. On that day Weiss walked out of the old criminal court building—then on its last legs as a courthouse—and headed toward the flower shop in a car. He couldn't have failed to pass the adjacent jail on Illinois Street, where the gallows had been set up for every Chicago hanging since 1872, when hangings had moved to the new prison from the old one in the Loop. The gallows, too, was on its last legs at the time; within months the State of Illinois would switch to the electric chair for its executions, against the objections of city officials who thought the chair was barbaric compared to a quick, clean hanging.

But the execution Weiss was heading for as he passed the spot that had been fatal for nearly a hundred men would not be quick or clean, and there was no due process behind it. Weiss was living proof that the threat of the death penalty wasn't much of a deterrent to crime for gangsters. No matter what method the State of Illinois used, he and his men were living under the same threat from much less thoughtful hands—people who cared little about whether punishments were cruel and unusual and even less about the right to a trial by a jury.

Weiss was riding to Schofield's in a Cadillac driven by Sam Peller; his bodyguard sat in the front seat. Another car heading to Schofield's carried William O'Brien, a Saltis defense attorney. All the men got out near Superior and State and began walking across State Street to reach the flower shop. As they crossed, the roar of machine guns erupted from a shop window above them.

Patrick Murray, the bodyguard, fell onto the sidewalk just in front of the door of Schofield's, dead before his head made contact with the pavement.

Weiss, hit by eight bullets, fell in the street; a shotgun blast, distinct from the typewriter rattle of the Thompson submachine guns, finished him off.

Sam Peller managed to fire a single pistol shot before getting a bullet in his groin, sending him reeling backwards toward the cathedral. William O'Brien was hit in the arm, the side, and the stomach as he raced for the safety of a stairwell that led to the basement of the flower shop.

The shooter reloaded and then fired at Peller and Benny Jacobs, another man on the scene, as they raced down State Street and around the corner of the cathedral.

The shooting lasted only seconds. Peller and Jacobs managed to stumble into a doctor's office on Cass Street, where their lives were saved. O'Brien remained in the stairwell until a passing woman told him there was a doctor's office a few doors down. He raced there and was eventually brought to Mercy Hospital, where doctors kept the four bullet wounds from killing him.

Weiss had been peppered with gunshots, including one that punctured his face below his left eye. He was alive but not conscious when the ambulance arrived; consciousness never returned, and Weiss slipped into death at Henrotin Hospital.

As for the killers, witnesses saw a couple of men jump from a window of the boardinghouse at 740 North State, one carrying a Tommy gun and the other carrying a couple of pistols. The guns were discarded in the alley as the two men ran off; they were never caught.

In the aftermath of the shooting, police found thirty-five empty machine-gun shells in a pile near the window of the boarding room, along with a few shot-gun shells and a used shot-gun. Cigarette butts—more than a hundred of them— littered the floor of the hotel room, indicating that the

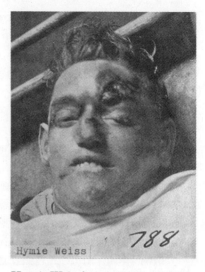

Hymie Weiss's gruesome remains
PUBLIC RECORD

killers had been holed up in the room for quite a long time. Near the shells was a freshly purchased hat whose tag indicated it had come from a dealer in Cicero—Caponeville.

It was easy enough for police to put the events together. Members of the Capone gang, fearing for their lives after the attack in Cicero and rueful of the notion that Weiss might be able to get Saltis off the hook and form a solid alliance with him, had set up camp in the boardinghouse, waited for their time to strike, then pounced when the opportunity presented itself. But there was no proof—nothing that could have sent a man to prison. There were no prints on the guns, and no way to connect them to their owners.

Naturally the chief of police ordered a reorganization of the police department "in order to run gangsters forever out of the city," a line that now struck Chicago as charming in its naïveté. No arrests were ever made, and the killing officially remained a mystery for the cold case files.

On October 12, the day after the killing, Capone called in representatives of the press and gave a statement.

"I'm sorry Weiss was killed," he said, "but I didn't have anything to do with it. I telephoned the detective bureau [and said] I'd come in if they wanted me, and they told me they didn't want me. I knew I'd be blamed for it, but why should I kill Weiss?"

"He was supposed to be your rival," a reporter pointed out.

But Capone said nothing.

He had learned by then that sometimes it was best to keep his mouth shut.

Days after the assassination, every policeman the *Tribune* could find said he was certain that Capone had ordered the killing, but given the lack of hard proof, none dared to arrest him. Another rival was dead, and Capone continued to walk the streets a free man.

CHAPTER ELEVEN

Peace in the City?

In the days immediately following the killing of Hymie Weiss, Capone made a very public call for a peace conference.

This would be no backroom deal in which Capone sent an emissary; this would be a public conference, one well publicized in the press. Capone was becoming a master of PR and probably saw the conference as a chance not only to make arrangements to stop the war that was bad for everyone's business, not to mention his personal safety, but also to portray himself to the public as a man of peace.

This was to be a respectable meeting, one that would be overseen by former mayor William Hale "Big Bill" Thompson, who was planning to run for mayor again that spring. Of course, by this point using "respectable" in the same sentence as "Big Bill Thompson" was already faintly ridiculous. He had spent his years out of office pretending to be on an expedition to discover some sort of South American tree-climbing fish. The "expedition" kept his name in the papers, despite his never getting

PEACE IN THE CITY?

close to South America. Soon Thompson would be staging debates with his political opponents for the press, with caged rats standing in for the absent opponents. That the gangsters all seemed to favor him as a mayoral candidate probably speaks volumes.

In the earliest portion of the meeting, Tony Lombardo spoke for Capone, and one Maxie Eisen spoke for what newspapers had already begun referring to as the "Moran-Drucci" gang now that Weiss was dead. Peace "delegates" were chosen: Capone, Lombardo, Ralph Sheldon, Frank Nitti, and Jake Guzik for the Capone gang; Bugs Moran, Vinnie Drucci, Max Eisen, and two other men for the North Siders.

The two other men, Barney Bertshchet and William Skidmore, were said to be reluctant but were convinced that by attending the conference, they were performing a valuable service in protecting the good name of the city of Chicago.

Terms of an armistice were laid down:

1. No more killings or beatings.
2. All past murders and shooting attributed to gunmen affiliated with Chicago and Cicero mobs will henceforth be looked on as closed incidents—no more revenge or reprisal.
3. All ribbing [gossip] between the factions by policemen or reporters would be disregarded.
4. Leaders of the factions would be held responsible for any violations of the peace pact and would be responsible for disciplining their members.

To ask that the shootings of Torrio, Weiss, and so many others be regarded as water under the bridge was a lot to ask. But Capone made an emotional appeal that seemed to sway everyone.

If Capone's own later description of the meeting is to be believed, he appealed to people's sense of humanity by holding up a picture of his son, stating that he wanted to stop the killings for his sake. "I couldn't stand hearing my little kid ask why I didn't stay home," he said. "I had been living in the Hawthorne Inn for fourteen months. . . . If it wasn't for him, I would have said, 'to hell with you fellows! We'll shoot it out.' But I couldn't say that, knowing it might mean they'd bring me home some night punctured with machine-gun fire." He told the skeptical gangsters that they were "making a shooting gallery out of a great business, and nobody's profiting by it. It's hard and dangerous work and when a fellow works hard in any line of business, he wants to go home and forget it. He doesn't want to be afraid to sit near a window or open a door. . . . There's plenty of beer business for everybody. Why kill each other over it?"

This vision of returning to Torrio's old philosophy seemed to appeal to everyone present, and the remarkable truce was agreed to.

A reporter later spoke of following members of rival gangs to the Bella Napoli cafe for an after-party, where they celebrated the dawn of a new day and acted like old friends.

"Remember that night when your car was chased by two of ours?" one man asked another.

"I sure do!" the other replied.

"We were going to kill you, but you had a woman with you." Both men laughed and drank like old buddies, which is how they were to think of one another from now on. From then on, Capone said, they would all do their business in their own territories; and when they met on the street, they would shake hands and say hello.

Tony the Greek

Many sources say the truce lasted for around seventy days, until the body of Capone ally Theodore Anton, alias Tony the Greek (often listed as the landlord of the Hawthorne Inn) was found dead on January 5, 1927. One version of events has Capone hearing a knock on the door that night and a voice announcing the knocker as Tony the Greek, going to the door to find no one there, and waking the next morning to the news that Tony had been taken for a ride, ending the truce.

In fact, though, by January 5 Tony had been missing for more than a month, and his disappearance had caused quite a stir in the press.

Tony the Greek was a former boxer who had used his winnings as a fighter to buy up real estate in Cicero. Officially he was owner of the Hawthorne Hotel, among several other establishments in the area. Like many other pugilists of the day, he had become friendly with a number of underworld types during his tenure in the ring. And when the gangsters moved into Cicero, he became good friends with Capone.

By the end of 1926 though, Tony was getting fed up with the troubles his gangland association brought him. Having his building shot up by a parade of cars full of machine-gunners was not exactly good for business; between those and the police raids, the Hawthorne Hotel had become something of a ghost town.

He tried changing the name of the Hawthorne to the Western Hotel to shake off the gang association, but the move was unsuccessful; business continued to lag. Some believe that the Capone gang got tired of hearing him whine and decided to get rid of him. Others say that North Siders thought he was too close to Capone and decided to get rid of him.

But his disappearance and death may not have had anything to do with the gangs at all. It's quite possible that the truce was still in effect and being respected.

On November 28, barely a month after the notorious peace conference, Tony left his house, notably wearing over a thousand dollars' worth of jewelry. On November 30 his wife reported to the police that he was missing. His friends suggested that he might have been killed while resisting a holdup, but police were quick to point out to reporters that the man was a close friend of "Scarface Al Caponi," and that such a man's disappearance almost *had* to have some connection to his ties to the vice lord.

On December 3 a young man noticed a pool of blood on Seeger Bridge, which ran over a drainage canal near suburban Des Plaines. Upon exploring the space beneath the bridge, he found a blood-drenched coat bearing the name of "T. Anton." Police promptly dragged the canal, but no body was found.

Clues continued to pile up as to what had happened. The next day police found a shallow grave near the bridge, along with a fully loaded automatic pistol believed to have belonged to Tony. Footprints—many made by bare feet—were found around the grave, and a pair of rubber boots were found stuck in the mud. What had happened was fairly apparent: Tony had been taken to the bridge and killed, and the killers had planned to bury the body in a shallow grave. However, as no body was found on the scene, police speculated that the killers had found the cold ground too difficult to dig out, forcing them to take the body someplace else.

A week later the body of a murdered man—shot three times and badly burned—was found alongside the road in a lonesome part of South Chicago Heights. On the basis of a cauliflower ear and twisted lip that were still identifiable on the brutalized man, relatives initially thought it was Tony, but Tony's dentist determined that the dead man's teeth didn't match Tony's dental records. It was later said that the body was that of a boxer whose killers had burned the body to prevent identification.

More than a month after Tony's disappearance, a body positively identified as his was found buried in a shallow grave in the suburb of Burnham. A paper bag had been drawn over the head, and the body had been buried under a pool of lime to aid in rapid decomposition. An empty bag nearby showed that the lime had been purchased from the Meyer Davis Company on Roosevelt Road.

Some have noted a similarity between the Anton murder and the plot of *The Mystery of Edwin Drood* by Charles Dickens. Dickens died before the book was finished, so no one really knows how it was to end, but the "orthodox" solution to the unfinished mystery is that John Jasper killed Edwin Drood, the story's namesake, and that the mystery would be solved when Drood's ring was found in a grave. Dickens set up clues that Jasper would bury the body in quicklime that would destroy the body but also noted that Drood was wearing a ring. The ring wouldn't decompose. This, as it turned out, was exactly how the body of Tony the Greek was identified. By the time the body was found, the lime had badly damaged the remains. The face was completely unrecognizable, aside from the still-visible cauliflower ears. But on what was left of the right hand of the dead man was a ring bearing the name Irene Tourin, the maiden name of Tony's wife. Aiding in the identification was the fact that the middle finger—the one on which he had worn a $1,500 ring—had been cut off and was missing.

Whether this was truly the end of the truce, or just an unrelated killing, remains a mystery to this day. The murder simply doesn't make sense if one views it as a gangland killing. Capone may have become annoyed with Tony's complaints about his business being shot up and raided, but even Capone wasn't the type to kill a friend because he was whining. The North Siders probably had little motivation to kill Tony either; he was Capone's friend, but Capone had lots of friends. As far as it is known, there was no strategic advantage to getting Tony the Greek out of the way.

Besides the lack of a motive, the method of getting rid of the body was unusual for gangsters. Very rarely had either gang taken any steps whatsoever to hide the bodies of its victims. Most were simply left in the pools of blood and gore where they fell, or shoved out of the car when they were done being taken for a ride. To kill someone, bring the body back to the car, and then bury it in lime was highly unusual.

Some pinpoint this as the first time the Chicago mob had tried to hide the body of a victim, but it seems likely that the man's friends had been right. This wasn't a mob killing but a simple holdup for the jewelry carried out by people who had no idea whom they were dealing with and that had gotten way out of hand.

Still, word went out around the world that the truce between the gangs was over. Though gang violence continued to be relatively low throughout the early days of 1927, there was a mayoral election coming up that spring.

And by then a local election in Chicago with no interference from the gangs was no local election at all.

Vinnie the Schemer and Big Bill

Upon the death of Hymie Weiss, newspapers had been quick to name George "Bugs" Moran as the new big shot of the North Side. "George Moran," wrote the *Tribune*, "now takes the scepter torn by murder first from the fist of Dean O'Banion, and lately from the grasp of Hymie Weiss, and he becomes the ruler of the bootleg domain of [the north side of] Chicago."

In a move that probably pushed Capone toward the peace conference gambit, word of the new leader was sent to Deputy Chief of Detectives John Stege, who told reporters he had learned that all the gangs of Chicago were now joining forces against Al Capone. There were, he said, now two gangs in town, not eight. Everyone by then was either a Capone man or a Moran man.

But Moran had seldom been mentioned as a major player in the press before; after O'Banion's demise, papers usually referred to the North Siders as a "Weiss-Drucci" gang.

So where did this leave Vinnie "The Schemer" Drucci? Why didn't *he* take up the "scepter?"

Drucci had never been a serious enough man to take the helm of the gang himself. Indeed, you might have even called the man more of a court jester, except that court jesters aren't usually as handy with firearms as the sadistic Drucci.

Drucci had earned his nickname by constantly coming up with bizarre schemes to increase the gang's power. Originally a jewel thief and safecracker, Drucci had first made a name for himself with his scheme to rob payphones by blasting them open and taking the change. By 1922 he was making the news (under the name Vincent "Skimmer" Drucci) after taking part in a spectacular car chase on Michigan Avenue. At the time he was already wanted for cracking a safe belonging to a woman who owned a tea shop. A couple of police sergeants spotted his car cruising through the lower North Side and began following him. Drucci recognized the officers right away and raced south down Michigan Avenue just as the two halves of the drawbridge over the river were being raised to let a steamer through. Drucci drove up the rising north half of the bridge and made a daring four-foot jump to the south half.

The police, not to be outdone, followed him, jumping the bridge on their own, even though the gap was wider by then, and caught up with Drucci while he sat in traffic. A crowd of Michigan Avenue onlookers watched in shock.

This was not the only time Drucci would capture the attention of Michigan Avenue. Besides a couple of firefights mentioned earlier, it was also here that he had his best times dressing up as a priest to compliment passers-by on their backsides. One time even O'Banion got in on the act, pretending to beat up on Drucci while he was in the priest outfit, helping to spread the word that O'Banion was crazy enough to beat the hell out of a priest.

One of the few Italians in the North Side mob, Drucci was known for his wild imagination. At various times he came up with plans to go to London to steal the crown jewels, to overthrow the US government, and, in October 1926, to actually go along with Capone's peace plan. It's often said that Drucci was the one who talked Moran into accepting the cease-fire, which in hindsight might have seemed just as crazy as any of Drucci's own schemes.

When 1927 rolled around, and with it a mayoral election, Drucci allegedly made plans to run for the office himself. This was quickly put down, but both North and South Side gangs were determined to stay involved in politics, since the mayor's attitude affected their business tremendously. William Dever had been trying his hardest to keep Chicago a dry town and clean the gangsters out of the city. It's generally agreed that his men's vigilance played a large part in pushing Capone and Torrio out of the city (for the most part) and into the suburbs, at least for a few years. Having a more sympathetic, and perhaps easier to bribe, mayor would be good for both gangs.

Big Bill Thompson, the most corrupt mayor Chicago ever had (which is really saying something) LIBRARY OF CONGRESS

When the new election rolled around, Dever was challenged by returning former mayor Big Bill Thompson, whose promise to make Chicago an "open city" was favored by both major gangs.

Thompson and Drucci were, in many ways, two peas in a pod. Both were given to grand schemes and general buffoonery, but while Drucci may have dreamed up ways to become mayor, Thompson actually pulled it off.

For his return in 1927, without being able to run as the "law and order" candidate while still promising an "open city," he hit on a particularly novel way to unify voters: convincing them that they were somehow being threatened by King George V of England. King George, he said, was plotting to take America back, starting by introducing "pro-English" textbooks into American schools and libraries. It sounds outrageous, but anti-British sentiment played well in Irish and German neighborhoods, which were abundant in Chicago.

Al Capone put a picture of Thompson up in his office and is said to have contributed at least a quarter of a million dollars to his reelection effort (though this may have just been a rumor spread by the opposition). When the election came around in April 1927, Drucci embarked on a typically harebrained scheme to make sure the Republican Big Bill Thompson was elected—by antagonizing the Democratic challenger's offices and workers with bombs and kidnappings.

On the day before the election, two Democratic headquarters in the lower North Side were firebombed (though there were no injuries), and general orders were given to the police to arrest any known troublemakers. Drucci, for his part, had recently raided the offices of Alderman Dorsey Crowe, a supporter of Mayor Dever, and was said to be working on a crazy scheme to kidnap Crowe and other Dever workers until the election was over.

But Drucci was among those picked up by the police acting on general orders. The arrest was made by Officer Daniel Healy, a police officer known to be particularly antagonistic toward gangsters. Drucci was carrying a .45 when they caught him. As they stood in the police station, Drucci objected to Healy holding him by the arm. An argument ensued, and Drucci called Healy "an ugly name" that has been lost to history (though several possibilities can be easily imagined).

Healy slapped Drucci, pulled out his gun, and said, "Call me that again and I'll let you have it."

The two men continued arguing as they got into a car and began heading toward the criminal court building, with Drucci and Healy taking the window seats in the back with another man between them.

"Go on, you kid copper," Drucci said as he got in. "I'll fix you for this."

Upon being told to shut his mouth, Drucci said, "You take your gun off and I'll kick hell out of you."

As the car began to move, Drucci kept it up, striking Healy upside the head and saying, "I'll take you and your tool."

He then began to reach for Healy's gun, shouting, "I'll fix you."

The car came to halt at Wacker Drive, facing the Clark Street Bridge. Healy grabbed the gun himself and fired four shots at Drucci. One bullet hit him in the left arm, another went into his right leg, and a third went into his abdomen.

Immediately the car's destination was changed from the criminal court building to Iroquois Hospital, which was just down Wacker Drive. From there Drucci was moved to a county hospital, where he was pronounced dead on arrival. He was thirty-one. Appropriately for a joker like Drucci, shots of his corpse in the morgue show his face fixed in something like a grin.

Attorneys for Drucci and the gangsters immediately tried to charge Healy with murder, but Chief of Detectives William Shoemaker assured reporters that a medal was being made ready for Healy and that Drucci had been shot while trying to take away an officer's gun.

Just about everyone felt the case was a little bit fishy. Oscar Wolff, the coroner, said he couldn't believe that armed officers couldn't have restrained Drucci without shooting him.

Drucci's wife, Cecelia, arrived at the morgue to identify the body, crying and calling him "my great big baby." She immediately made plans for a grand funeral to put him in the league of O'Banion. He was eventually laid up in a shiny $10,000 casket of aluminum and silver, surrounded by $30,000 in flowers. He was carried to a vault in Mount Carmel with full military honors (he had served in the US Navy during World War I) after a funeral attended by more than a thousand at Sbarbaro's chapel at 708 North Wells, right near one of the offices that had been bombed. "A policeman murdered him," said Cecilia at the time, "but we sure gave him a grand funeral."

Following Drucci's death the police took every possible precaution for the upcoming election, stationing guards at every voting place and office. In the end, Drucci's candidate, Big Bill Thompson, defeated Dever handily, meaning there would be new chiefs of police and new men in all the big city jobs. Big Bill said he got elected because of his opposition to King George V, but the newspapers knew otherwise: The people of Chicago wanted an open city, not a mayor who actually tried to enforce the prohibition laws.

Even if it meant ending up with a screwball like Big Bill.

CHAPTER TWELVE

A New Chicago

Big Bill Thompson was certainly no friend of Prohibition and openly flouted the law, stating that he was "wetter than the middle of the Atlantic Ocean."

But Big Bill Thompson had bigger ambitions than simply being mayor of Chicago when he reclaimed the office in the spring of 1927. He honestly believed he had a chance to be nominated for president of the United States in 1928, and to that end he actually kept up the battle against the bootleggers to bolster his image. Capone had expected that under Thompson he'd be able to operate in the city with impunity—and he did in fact come close. But by this time Capone was a known public enemy, and every time a murder took place in Chicago, his was the first name suggested as the killer, whether there was any earthly reason to connect him to it or not.

By December 1927 Capone was fed up and complained to reporters that people had tried to hang every crime except the Great Chicago Fire on him. On December 5 Capone brought reporters into his headquarters at the Metropole Hotel and announced that he was leaving town.

"I'm leaving for St. Petersburg tomorrow," he said. "Let the worthy citizens of Chicago get their liquor the best they can. I'm sick of the job—it's a thankless one and full of grief. I don't know when I'll get back, if ever. But it won't be before the holidays, anyway."

Capone sat in an easy chair, wearing a new hunting suit and sporting a week's growth of beard on his chin, which he had grown on a recent hunting trip in the North Woods. As he sat he portrayed himself, yet again, as the best man in Chicago.

"I've been spending the best years of my life as a public benefactor," said the twenty-eight-year-old Capone. "I've given people the light pleasures, shown them a good time, and all I get is abuse—the existence of a hunted animal. I'm called a killer. Well, I'm going away now. I guess murder will stop. There won't be any more booze. You won't be able to find a crap game, even, let alone a roulette wheel or a faro game. . . . Public service is my motto. Ninety-nine percent of the people in Chicago drink and gamble. I've tried to serve them decent liquor and square games. But I'm not appreciated."

The reporters milled about the room, and Capone kept on talking.

"Say," he said. "The coppers won't have to lay all the gang murders on me now. Maybe they'll find a new hero for the headlines. It would be a shame, wouldn't it, if while I was away they would forget about me and find a new gangland chief? I wish all my friends and enemies a merry Christmas and a happy New Year. That's all they'll get from me. . . . I hope I don't spoil anybody's Christmas by not sticking around. My wife and my mother hear so much about what a terrible criminal I am; it's getting too much for them, and I'm just sick of it all myself."

On and on Capone talked of what a hard life he had. And though it's hard to feel sorry for a ruthless killer, it's also easy to imagine that being everyone's idea of the world's biggest criminal brought with it a unique set of headaches.

"Today I got a letter from a woman in England," he said. "Even over there I'm seen as a gorilla. She offered to buy my passage to London if I'd kill some neighbors she'd been having a hard time with."

This was also probably the conference at which Capone made perhaps his most famous utterance: "They call Al Capone a bootlegger. Yes, it's bootleg while it's on the trucks, but when your host at the club, in the locker room, or on the Gold Coast hands it to you on a silver salver, it's hospitality."

And so Capone took off. A *Tribune* headline the next day read "'You Can All Go Thirsty' is Big-Hearted Al's Adieu."

But Florida was not Capone's first stop. He first went to Los Angeles, where the authorities promptly ordered him to get out of town.

Within a week and a half, he was on a train heading back to Chicago, and the Chicago police were planning a stakeout. They would be waiting at every train station, and upon his return they were going to arrest him for unlawful weapon possession. Sergeant Healy, the man who had killed Drucci, was among the officers stationed and ready.

Capone was in fact briefly jailed upon his arrival in Joliet. A few of his men arrived at the train station there ahead of him but were arrested when the bulges in their pockets gave them away as gangsters. When Capone stepped off the train, the Joliet chief of police was waiting.

"You're Al Capone," he said.

"Pleased to meet you," said Capone.

He was promptly arrested and was briefly put into a cell with a couple of unkempt minor prisoners. He promptly paid their fines with cash from his pockets to get them out of his way. While in his now-private cell, he spoke to the police about his trip.

"The newspapers began printing things about me while I was just being a tourist," he moaned. "I went over [to] some of the movie studios in Hollywood. That's a grand racket. I looked at the stars' homes. I think Mary Pickford's old home was nicer than the one she lives in now."

He noted though that he didn't make any plans to settle in Los Angeles, for a reason that has never been given by anyone else at any point in history: It rained too often there. "It rained two days while I was in Los Angeles," he said of the famously dry city.

He was released from Joliet after only eight hours and taken by car to his mother's Chicago house, where he was safe from the Chicago police as long as he didn't go outside. "We haven't any specific charge against him," Chief of Detectives William O'Connor admitted, "and we won't break into a home to get him. I have instructed any bureau squads that see him on the street to pick him up and take him to jail."

Police surrounded the house, with orders to arrest anyone who came or went. Capone could do nothing but pace back and forth, growling. Eventually, on December 22, he came out in a car and drove to Joliet to face the charges of unlawful weapon possession for which he'd been arrested.

"Maybe this will be a lesson to you," the judge told him.

"Yes, Judge, it certainly will," said Capone with a smile. "I'll never tote a gun again in Joliet."

He was fined $1,000, plus court costs, and peeled some cash—a $1,000 bill and a number of hundreds—out of his pocket and handed it over.

The clerk tried to hand Capone $10.20 in change, and Capone smiled and handed it back.

"Just drop it in the Salvation Army fellow's kettle out there and tell him Al Capone sent it," he said.

Days later he left Chicago for Florida, where he intended to set up camp in Miami. Again he was besieged by reporters and the public. This time, to all appearances, Capone was determined to operate on the level. He and a lieutenant walked right into the office of the chief of police.

"Let's lay the cards on the table, Chief," he said. "You know who I am and where I came from. I just want to ask a question: Do I stay or must I get out?"

After Capone assured the chief he had no intention of opening a gambling parlor in Florida, the chief told him he could stay as long as he behaved. As soon as he got the word, Capone called in the reporters and told them he would be sending for his wife and son to come stay with him in Miami for the winter and that he may even buy some property there.

"I've been hounded and pushed around for the last two days," he said. "It began when somebody heard I was in town. All I have to say is that I'm orderly. Talk about Chicago gang stuff is just bunk."

Capone wound up staying well beyond the winter. With a seemingly endless supply of cash, he purchased property and built an estate for himself. He continued to be hounded by the police and was occasionally brought in to testify that he had no role in various slayings that continued to take place in connection to his gang, but generally he seemed to settle into the life of a rich man on Palm Island. It may have looked to some as though his gangster days were behind him and that he'd taken Torrio's cue to get out while the getting was good.

But in September 1928 a killing took place in Chicago that couldn't have failed to attract Capone's notice.

Murder at Dearborn and Madison

One of Capone's first orders of business as big shot of the Chicago outfit had been to install Tony Lombardo as head of the powerful Unione Siciliana (which by 1928 newspapers regularly referred to as simply "the Mafia.") Lombardo had promptly opened up membership to non-Sicilians, making Capone eligible to join at last.

On September 7, 1928, while Capone was in Florida, Lombardo was walking through the Loop in downtown Chicago with two bodyguards. He was ambushed by gunmen at the corner of Madison and Dearborn who shot him in the back of the head, killing him instantly. The crowded intersection went into a panic, and the killers made an escape through the crowd.

Police immediately went looking for Capone (who was rumored to be back in town), but Capone was found to be in hiding in Florida, fearing for his life even though he was miles away. If Lombardo was a target, then so was he, and the men who killed Lombardo could take a train south easily enough.

Also in hiding was the Aiello gang from the North Side, which had been vying for control of the Unione for some time and had also been trying to kill Capone for quite a while. In fact, Joe Aiello is said to have offered a chef $30,000 to poison Capone's soup.

Police tried to say the killing of Lombardo was just another gang killing, but the papers knew it wasn't. "[The death of Lombardo] meant a war to the death between the most powerful of the Sicilian rulers of Chicago," said the *Tribune*. "It meant that Capone was a marked man, and that numerous murders are likely to follow. . . . It may mean a shifting of the political ownership of thousands of Sicilian votes. It is considered the most important murder in Chicago since Sicilians invaded the floral shop of Dean O'Banion and killed him."

Also shot in the assault was Joseph Ferraro, a bodyguard. Police found him lying on the ground, trying to wave a gun around. They stepped on his wrist to disarm him and tried to get him to talk.

"You're going to die," an officer said. "Who shot you?"

The dying man of course said nothing.

The truce was over for real now, and any plans Capone had to retire in comfort and safety were smashed. Action would be required.

CHAPTER THIRTEEN

"They're Full of Dead Men in There!"

On Valentine's Day 1929 a woman on the 2100 block of North Clark Street saw policemen enter the SMC Cartage Company and then saw them emerge with a couple of men holding their hands up, like a liquor raid. The men got into a police car and swerved recklessly around a passing trolley.

"Of course," she later said, "I got a little curious." She had, after all, heard a whole lot of noise coming out of the garage. What the heck was going on?

She found the door stuck and went back across the street to the rooming house she ran, where she enlisted one of the roomers to go investigate for her. He pried the door open, then stepped inside. A moment later he emerged, his face as white as ashes and frozen in a look of terror.

"They're full of dead men in there!" he shouted.

In the garage seven men lay in one big pool of blood, and from somewhere amid the dark scene of the carnage, a distinct, ghostly voice had called out, "Who's there?"

Aftermath of the St. Valentine's Day Massacre: "They're full of dead men in there!" LIBRARY OF CONGRESS

One of the seven men was still alive, so the voice was probably his. But with the other six men in the garage lying dead in a pool of blood, guts, and brains, the place certainly could have been haunted already. Some in the neighborhood have said the site has been haunted ever since.

Police were called in to the ghastly scene at once.

Among the first officers on the scene was Tom Loftus, who had known the still-living man, Frank Gusenberg, for years. He looked down at Frank, who had been shot more than a dozen times but was still breathing, and tried to get him to tell what happened.

"For God's sake," said Gusenberg. "Get me to a hospital."

"I want you to explain this shooting, Frank!" shouted Loftus.

"I refuse to tell," said Gusenberg.

Around him, blood was pooling into the drain, and six corpses were spread across the ground. Their own guns, pulled from their pockets, were on the floor beside them. It was easy to imagine what had happened. A group of men dressed as police officers had lined the seven men up against the wall as though it had been a routine liquor raid, relieved them of their guns, and then mowed them down from behind with machine guns. Two men had also been shot in the face with shotguns—the typical "finishing move" of a gangland execution.

When the other police arrived, they quickly realized that the dead men were all members of the Moran gang. History would remember their assassination as the St. Valentine's Day Massacre.

The Never-ending Investigation Begins

Entering the SMC cartage company from a door on Clark Street back in 1929, you found yourself in a long, narrow garage extending a hundred feet or so into the alley. The dingy spot had been a frequent rendezvous point for the Moran gang and their beer trucks and was now crowded with police officers and reporters. Officers told the reporters that they believed the Moran gang had fallen on hard times. The booze racket wasn't as profitable as it had been before, and many of their gambling establishments had recently been shut down.

Detectives combed through the men's pockets though and indicated that the men were not exactly hard up. Lt. John L. Sullivan handed a pile of cash—$447—and a diamond ring to Lt. Otto Erlanson. "Body of Number One," he said.

Body Number One was Pete Gusenberg, Frank's brother. Pete had been in and out of prison for burglary jobs since 1906, including a three-year stint from 1923 to 1926 for his role in a mail robbery at Dearborn Station. Since emerging from jail, he had been known as a member of the Moran gang and had been taken into custody several times when police went around rounding up the usual suspects. The most recent occasion had been only a week before.

Sullivan moved to the next body and announced that it was Albert Weinshank. Contents of the dead man's pockets included $18 in cash, a diamond ring, and a bankbook that gave his name as A. R. Shanks. Police believed he had only just joined the gang as part of Moran's scheme to take over the cleaning and dying industry in Chicago.

Body Number Three was identified first as Adam Heyer, then as John Snyder or John Hayes. "He was the brains of the Moran mob," someone told the chief. He'd been in prison a few times for robbery but had been free since about 1923 and apparently worked as a bookkeeper for the Moran gang. He was carrying nearly $1,400 in cash when he was killed.

Next to him lay a man in brown overalls, a stark contrast to the men in pinstriped suits but just as dead as the rest of them. The man was John May, a former safe-blower who had been trying to go straight to provide for his seven children. He was no longer a member of the gang but was paid to work on their trucks as a mechanic. His pockets contained a few bucks and a couple of St. Christopher medals. The medals had been kept in a case, but a bullet had gone right through the case and damaged the medals. May's was one of the bodies that had taken a shotgun blow to the face—the whole left part was obliterated.

Body Number Five, next to May, was Reinhardt Schwimmer, who was not actually part of the gang but was only a twenty-eight-year-old failed optometrist who enjoyed hanging around with gangsters. He enjoyed bragging to his friends that he could have them killed if he wanted to, which probably made him a lot less popular than he imagined. He had probably been thrilled to be lined up against the wall next to such men as Pete Gusenberg, but now there were sixteen bullet wounds in his back. Seven bullets would later be removed from his chest. Another bullet had gone through his head and caused extensive laceration of the brains some people say he must have lacked to go around with gangsters like that.

Beside Schwimmer lay James Clark, Body Number Six; $681 was found in his clothes. Clark was a brother-in-law to Moran and known as a ruthless killer.

"Four of the bodies have overcoats," noted a detective. "Clark in undercoat only, and May in overalls. Count the hats."

There were seven hats along the ground, the seventh presumably belonging to Frank Gusenberg, who had been taken to the hospital without his headgear.

At the back of the room, a large Alsatian shepherd said to be named Highball was chained to a beer truck. Police reporters noted that the dog looked vicious but scared. Later reports said the dog was hysterical and that it was his barking that attracted the neighbors, but reporters at the time said the dog wasn't barking at all. He seemed mystified that so many men dared to walk near him, but he remained calm.

Still, detectives warned reporters not to get too close to the dog. "Seven men died like dogs," one reporter said, "but the dog lives."

Most of the bullets fired had hit their marks, but there were bullet holes all over the wall. A saw that had been hanging over a bench had been cut in half by a spray of bullets, an ironic end for such a tool.

There had clearly been no struggle; the guns found on the ground were all unfired. Police were amazed that seven such men could have been lined up against a wall without putting up a fight. The first witness to come forth, Mrs. Alphonsine Morin (whose names, in a bit of cosmic coincidence, were remarkably close to the first and last names of Alphonse Capone and George Moran), told the police about seeing two or three men in plainclothes being led out of the garage, hands in the air, by a couple of men in police uniforms.

"Quite simple," said Chief Egan. "They'd never have got that gang to line up unless they came in police uniforms. They wouldn't have got into the garage unnoticed, but it would appear that as policemen they walked in and surprised the gang sitting there and waiting for a message or for orders. For policemen, the gang would line up and face the wall, and I suppose the fake policemen disarmed them before they lined them up. Then when the stage was set, perhaps the other killers came in [through the back] and they took aim and started the machine gun and fired the shotguns and then as a precaution against trouble if they should meet policemen coming out, two or three of the killers put up their hands to indicate [that] they were prisoners in custody of police."

So the mystery of what had happened sorted itself out, but several mysteries about the massacre still hung heavy in the air. Who had shot these men, and why? It was particularly notable that Bugs Moran himself had not been present—later reports and stories claimed he had been on his way but had seen the police car pull up and ducked into a coffee shop to avoid getting caught up in a raid.

Why had the killers made the hit on this spot in the first place?

George "Bugs" Moran, the man who got away PUBLIC RECORD

Why had *all* the men been shot?

Why hadn't they waited for Moran? Wasn't he, as leader of the gang, the intended target?

And who had the killers been?

The only chance the world had to find out who the shooters were lay in the hands of Frank Gusenberg, who was rushed to the hospital. Doctors were able to stabilize him but held out no hope that he would survive. Once the doctors were finished, police asked him again to tell what had happened.

"Nobody shot me," Gusenberg told them. Other reports indicated that he said, "They were policemen."

He died minutes later. If he'd had any clue who the shooters were, he took that information to his grave.

What Happened?

Over the years, new theories as to what happened, and why, have come and gone every few months, and none of them seems to satisfy every historian. The bottom line that every investigator needs to remember is that nothing about the massacre really makes any sense. Why in the world would so many members of the gang, including Moran himself, have been meeting in the garage? Meeting a liquor shipment wouldn't have required nearly so many of the men.

And why wasn't Moran killed, anyway?

The simplest explanation—the idea that most theories revolve around—is that Capone, giving orders from his Florida hideaway, had brought in outside help in the form of men who wouldn't be recognized by the North Siders but who didn't know Moran very well themselves. Perhaps lookouts stationed in rooming houses across from the garage had seen seven men enter the building and, mistaking one of them for Moran, called in the hit. The killers had entered, lined the men up, and said "Which one of you is Bugs Moran?" When no one answered, the killers, now joined by some men who had come in through the back, simply shot all seven of them.

If that was the case, it was a remarkable showing of pure stupidity. Such a display brought down a lot of extra heat on gangsters everywhere.

Cops had immediately assumed that the massacre had been Capone's doing, but Capone himself was certainly not on the scene at the time. He was still in Miami, living like a king on his estate and trying to get a dog racing track started. The morning of the massacre, he had (conveniently) been meeting with officials to talk about the recent killing of Frankie Yale, Tony Lombardo's New York equivalent.

By then Capone had set himself up in a stately pleasure palace on Palm Island that would have been the envy of Kublai Khan. Newspaper photos showed him wearing a bathing suit while watching a boxing match on a ring that had been set up on the estate. A few days after the massacre, he was entertaining something like eighty guests, who he treated with all due hospitality. He was all smiles as he moved—seldom stopping even for a second—through the crowd.

On February 19, less than a week after the massacre, papers reported that it seemed as though every bootlegger, gambler, and gangster in Chicago had migrated to Miami. The *Tribune* estimated that five hundred of "our most notorious citizens" had gone to Florida. Hotel rates doubled at once. Gangsters who would talk at all explained that there was a lot of "heat" in Chicago.

Today rumor has it that Capone told reporters it had been Moran himself behind the killings. Various legends have him saying, "Only Moran kills guys like that," or

"They don't call him 'Bugs' for nothing." Other rumors have it that Moran hit things more squarely on the head, saying, "The only guy who kills guys like that is Al Capone." These quotes became a part of the Capone legend, despite the fact that no one is actually sure that either Capone or Moran ever said them. The truth is that *none* of the gangs usually killed guys like *that*. Lining seven men up and killing them, execution-style, was a departure from their usual methods of drive-bys, ambushes, and one-way rides.

That Capone's men had been behind the job seemed obvious enough. Capone had stopped making regular phone calls to Chicago some time before, but it was later found that calls had been placed to his estate from the Congress Hotel on Michigan Avenue shortly before and after the massacre. The Moran gang had recently been trying to muscle into Capone-controlled speakeasies, and no one could forget that the Gusenberg brothers had made a few very public attempts on the life of Jack McGurn, who by now was Capone's main hit man. And Capone's organization might have wanted to take revenge on the North Siders for the death of Tony Lombardo.

McGurn, for his part, had an alibi: He had been locked up in a hotel room with a blond showgirl the whole morning of the massacre. And besides, as he noted himself, it would have done him no good to dress up as a cop; the Gusenbergs would have recognized him and killed him right away.

But in those dizzying days right after the massacre, Capone's men weren't the *only* suspects. On February 16 the police announced that they planned to arrest several gunmen from Detroit.

All the information the police could obtain indicated that most of the Moran gang's booze had lately been imported from Canada via the Purple Gang, a group from Detroit, and police suspected that the Purple Gang had been involved in the shooting. However, their theory didn't seem to hold up; none of the pictures of the Detroit men could be identified by witnesses who saw the killers, or by the women who rented rooms to men believed to be the lookouts.

Still, clues supporting various theories continued to come in. H. Wallace Caldwell, president of the board of education, became an important witness. Minutes before the massacre Caldwell had seen the police car carrying the killers. He had noticed it because it collided with a Beaver Paper Company truck after running a red light but waved them off and kept driving. Moments later he heard the sound of gunshots coming from the nearby garage.

Unlike most witnesses, Caldwell had gotten a good enough look at the men to state that one of them was missing a front tooth. He had also been able to note the first few numbers on the license plate—321.

On February 21 the smoldering wreck of the car believed to be the police car used by the killers was found in a garage at 1723 North Wood, where it had been cut apart and burned. The garage had been rented on February 12 by a man named Frank Rogers of 1859 North Avenue. That address was deserted, but right next door stood the Circus Cafe, the North Avenue hangout of the Capone-aligned Circus Gang, the group that had given McGurn his start—and where three machine-gunners were now promptly arrested. Across the street stood the former home of Pasqualino Lolordo, who had taken up leadership of the Unione Siciliana after Lombardo had been killed (and who had promptly been killed as well).

All this, though, put the police no closer to finding the man with the missing tooth. Police had assumed the man in question was Fred Burke, a member of the Egan's Rats, a St. Louis gang that Capone was said to refer to as the "American Boys." Burke had been known to dress as a cop on crime sprees before, and he was missing a tooth. He had gone into hiding but was found on a farm two years later and captured without a fight. But he was only put on trial for another murder for which the evidence was stronger. He was never tried for his role in the massacre, though many believe him to be the triggerman. Still, there was no solid way to connect him to the stolen police car.

Even with all the clues pointing elsewhere, the top of the police's lists of suspects remained the most obvious —men working for the Capone outfit. On February 27, despite his "blond alibi," Jack McGurn was taken into custody. Of all the killers in town, he was the one with the most obvious motives for wanting the deadly Gusenberg brothers out of his way: Police said they had made two attempts on his life. He was taken into custody from his hideout in the Stevens Hotel, where he had been living with Louise Rolfe, his girlfriend, and was picked out of a lineup by two witnesses at the police station and identified as one of the killers. His connection to Maddox and the Circus Gang was noted as well.

McGurn was held for some time, but his alibi held up. And when he married Miss Rolfe, the state lost its chance to use her as a witness, since wives could not be made to testify against their husbands.

Among the others charged and briefly held were John Scalise and Albert Anselmi, Capone's major hit men, both of whom had not only beaten the promise of the gallows for their killing of police officers on the day Mike Genna was slain but had now been released from prison. Neither had ever been big shots in the brains department and were exactly the kinds of men who might have shot all seven of the cornered rivals, even if Moran wasn't among them, no matter how much heat such a stupid move would bring down on the gang.

If it *was* their fault the massacre had become such a fiasco, not just another hit, it might explain why they were found dead three months later.

Byron Bolton's Tale

In 1935 FBI agents raided an apartment on the North Side and arrested several people for their connection to the Ma Barker gang, a group of burglars and bank robbers who had been wreaking havoc across the Midwest for years. Among them was Byron Bolton, a relative unknown who had at one time been a member of Egan's Rats, the "American Boys." When Bolton was brought into custody, agents were allegedly shocked to hear him admit his role in the St. Valentine's Day Massacre.

Whether Bolton was telling the truth, or whether he really even told the story at all, remains a major controversy. His story was first broken in the *Chicago American,* a William Randolph Hearst–run tabloid that was notorious for printing wild rumors as fast as they could be dreamt up. Sources given for the story were vague at best.

According to the story, Bolton said he had met with a number of men, including Capone, to plot Moran's murder in the fall of 1928. That winter he and another man had rented a room on Clark Street, where they stayed for a few weeks staking out the SMC cargo company. On Valentine's Day he mistook one of the seven men who entered the garage for Moran and called in the hit to men stationed at the Circus Cafe. In his version of the story, only plainclothes men had been seen walking into the garage from his vantage point; anyone dressed as a cop would have come in from the back. The killers were most likely unknown small-timers, though Claude Maddox, boss of the Circus Gang of North Avenue, was among them.

The hit, Bolton supposedly said, had been a terrible mistake, and Capone had nearly killed him over it.

Various bits of evidence seemed to back up the story, including statements from Moran's friends and the widow of another man said to have been involved in the planning. However, most of these stories seem to have been published based only on secondhand accounts, and the full stories were only ever published in the Chicago tabloid and a true crime magazine. The FBI never acted to prosecute Bolton (possibly because they didn't feel they had jurisdiction in the case); anyway, by the time of his capture, nearly every man Bolton listed as being involved had been killed already. The six years that had passed was a long time in the gang world.

Revenge?

One theory that never quite died was that Gusenberg had been telling the truth when he said that police officers had been the shooters. Witnesses stated there was a gun rack mounted in the back of the car, indicating that it was a real police car, not just a regular car that had been painted up a little. And Bolton's story caught the eye of Frank T. Farrell, who wrote a recently discovered letter to FBI head J. Edgar Hoover describing, he said, what had *really* happened that day.

Farrell's story, publicized to the world years later by Jonathan Eig in *Get Capone,* brought in a whole new angle. In November 1928 William Davern, the son of a police officer, had been shot in a firefight in the kitchen of the C and O Restaurant at 509 North Clark. His bleeding body was taken down the back by car to Rush and Austin (Hubbard), where it was dumped. Still breathing, he worked his way to a phone box meant to make calls to the fire department and called for help.

In the hospital, as he lay dying over the course of thirty-one long days, his family had plenty of time to try to get him to talk. According to the story Farrell told before his death on December 30, six weeks prior to the massacre, he told his cousin the names of the killers. One of them was one of the Gusenberg brothers.

The cousin, William "Three Fingered Jack" White, was an old safecracker who had somehow lost two fingers on one hand in a job (or possibly a boyhood accident, depending on whom you believe). He had worked with the Gusenbergs before, supposedly dressing them as cops for burglary jobs, but when one of them killed his cousin, he made up his mind to get revenge.

Apparently White enlisted Sgt. William Davern, a police officer and the father of the dead man, to help with the raid. It would have been he who furnished the police car and possibly the uniforms, and maybe even a couple of actual cops. And he would have certainly been able to keep the police investigation from getting too close to the truth.

The story presents an elegant solution to the mystery, but as with so many other possible solutions, it doesn't clear up all the loose ends. What about the man with the missing tooth? Why was so much found that connected Maddox and McGurn to the crime? And of course there's the big one: Why were so many of them in the garage in the first place? And why had they killed *all* of them, not just the Gusenbergs?

Perhaps most importantly, how the heck could the dying Davern have gotten word to Three Fingered

Jack? After all, he was in jail at the time. This perhaps is the most telling argument against the story, though various attempts to explain that Jack briefly escaped have been made.

In any case, the FBI couldn't follow up on the letter when they received it in the 1930s. Three Fingered Jack had been shot to death a couple of years before. Claude Maddox was a suspect in the killing (though witnesses pointed to Klondike O'Donnell). The Farrell story is just one more twist in the mystery of the massacre that will continue to puzzle historians for years to come.

Capone's Own Revenge

Whether or not Capone had anything to do with the massacre, everyone in Chicago *assumed* that he had, and stories like this began chipping away at his image as a "Robin Hood" character and made him look like the "punk hoodlum" the FBI considered him. The orthodox explanation of the massacre was, and remained, that Jack McGurn had planned the massacre on Capone's orders, using men such as Clause Maddox of the Circus Gang, "Murder Twins" John Scalise and Albert Anselmi, and perhaps a couple of men brought in from St. Louis or Detroit who would not be recognized by the North Siders.

It's entirely likely that even if the whole thing *had* been just as big a mystery to him as it was to anyone else, Capone would have suspected that Scalise and Anselmi had been involved. And, perhaps against his better judgment, he might have decided to take their punishment into his own hands a few months later, especially after word got back to him that the two men had hatched yet *another* harebrained scheme: a plot to kill him and take over as heads of the operations.

Like most of the other major killings in Chicago gangland history, exactly what happened to Scalise and Anselmi remains a bit of a mystery, but this much is known: On May 7, 1929, not quite three months after the gruesome massacre, three bodies were found along a lonely stretch of road in Hammond Indiana, right near Wolf Lake, one of the city's most notable unofficial body dumps. Two corpses were slumped in the back seat of a car; the third was lying in the road, forty feet away.

It appeared as though the men had been shot to death elsewhere, and that the killers had then taken the bodies out of Hammond to leave them someplace safely away from the scene of the crime. Each had bullet wounds from pistol shots to the head and chest, and they had all been badly beaten, apparently with the butt ends of the guns or baseball bats. License plates on the "death car" identified it as the vehicle that had been stolen from Jamers Cerny, a South Side contractor, a week before.

Frank McNamara, the chief physician at the prison, said he'd never before seen bodies so badly damaged.

It took some time to determine that one of the bodies was that of Joseph "Hop Toad" Guinta, a man who had been aspiring toward leadership of the Unione Siciliana. But the other two men were almost immediately identified as John Scalise and Albert Anselmi, the notorious Murder Twins. They had beaten the gallows a few years earlier but had been cut down by men who couldn't be talked out of killing because of anything a lawyer told them or anything a jury decided.

Instantly the police pinned the blame on Bugs Moran, saying the killing of the three men had been revenge for the St. Valentine's Day Massacre, which authorities at the time believed to be partly the work of Scalise and Anselmi, though the two had been released under bond, along with McGurn, while the state worked its way through the investigation and tried to gather evidence.

The next day though, informants told the cops they had it all wrong. The men had been killed by Sicilians as part of the ongoing power struggle that revolved around control of the Unione Siciliana. According to these unnamed but apparently well-informed sources, the three men had been lured out to a roadhouse in Indiana by men they believed to be their friends to celebrate Guinta's rise to control of the Unione.

With four other men they sat around a table that groaned under the weight of rich food and wine. The three marked men had eaten and drunk themselves into something of a stupor. Once they were weak and exhausted, a signal was given, and the men were secured to their chairs. At that point the beatings and shootings began.

Battle for control of the Unione had been a deadly game for some time; leaders tended not to last long. After Lombardo's shocking murder at Dearborn and Madison, it was said to have been Scalise who put in Pasquale Lolordo as the man to take his place.

In January 1929, a month before the massacre, three men came into Lolordo's home and sat at his table, where they ate and drank with him before shooting him to death. As usual, the police were unsure who the killers were, but they had one suspect in mind: Joe Aiello, head of a North Side gang who had supposedly been trying to kill Capone for years after a brief stint as one of his friends years before. When police showed Mrs. Lolordo a picture of Aiello, she screamed.

Aiello had also been fingered as a possible suspect in the massacre, and local gangsters who believed him responsible seemed to have it in for him. In the weeks after the massacre, his store had been bombed, and police said that there had been several attempts made to assassinate him.

Scalise seemed to have it in for Aiello. A week before the Hammond, Indiana, incident, a meeting of gang leaders was apparently held in Cleveland in which the killers once again sought a cessation of hostilities. But according to reports, Scalise refused to enter into any peace pact before the killings of Lombardo and Lolordo had been avenged. Someone in the group had been a rat; the meeting ended with twenty-one men being arrested after police broke in.

Scalise's insistence that Lolordo's death be avenged made Aiello a marked man. And in this version of events, Aiello decided to act, taking both men down along with Guinta, the new head of the Unione, bringing his own record of killing Unione leaders up to at least three.

Guinta was still only the nominal, not official, head of the Unione, but he was given the sort of funeral appropriate to the Unione president. An expensive silver-bronze casket (valued at $5,000) was purchased, and more than a dozen floral pieces were delivered to his home. This was modest compared to some earlier presidents' funerals, to be sure, but certainly more of a show than was given to Scalise and Anselmi. Their bodies were sent to Sicily for burial; no flowers were sent with them.

The theory that Aiello had been the killer of the three seemed to satisfy most people, but remarkably he was never charged. He got out of town briefly, then came back to Chicago at the end of May, telling everyone that he was just a businessman. "I never bother any one else, and I just want to be let alone," he told everyone. Police let him go, apparently satisfied enough with his story (or at least with their own lack of evidence), and somewhat remarkably he was soon head of the Unione Siciliana—though he would be shot dead himself the next year.

Years later another version of the story of what had happened to the men became popular. According to this now-famous version of events, Aiello had convinced Scalise, Anselmi, and Guinta that Chicago would be a better place for all of them if Capone was out of the way. With the big guy dead, they themselves could take over the Unione and the outfit. But Capone got wind of the plot through his bodyguard, Frankie Rio. Perhaps already fuming that Scalise and Anselmi had brought so much heat down on him for their supposed role in the St. Valentine's Day Massacre, Capone returned to the Chicago area against his better judgment, and it was he who had lured the three men into the banquet and he who had beaten them to a bloody pulp with a baseball bat.

Whether Capone could even have been in Chicago at all is an open question—a week and a half later he was in custody at Moyamensing Prison in Philadelphia. He had apparently gone to Atlantic City to orchestrate another "peace pact," attended, it's said, by Aiello, Frank McErlane, Joe Saltis, Bugs Moran, and John Torrio himself, coming out of hiding for a brief reunion. The idea of all these men sitting at a table together under any circumstance seems astonishing. But the pieces seem to fit.

All in One Room

According to stories published in Chicago papers based on what Capone later told the police, he had been trying to orchestrate such a peace conference for some time, but Moran and the North Siders had refused any such meeting until Anselmi and Scalise were out of the picture. These, the North Siders said, were the men who had broken the last peace pact. Now that they had been eliminated, the conference was possible.

This *does* give Capone another possible motive for orchestrating their murder, if not actively participating in it himself. Having lost a couple hundred thousand bucks at the races, he needed the peace pact in order to get his business back to being as profitable as it had been when there wasn't all the shooting to deal with. His own gang, including Frank "The Enforcer" Nitti, was said to be getting annoyed that they were having to work so hard in Chicago, where profits were down, while Capone lived in luxury down on Palm Island.

The story of the ill-fated Cleveland meeting a few weeks before was retold, but this time with a twist: At that meeting, it was now said, Capone had quietly agreed to have Scalise and Anselmi eliminated. Three days later the men were killed, opening the door for another peace pact. According to Capone himself, shortly after the Murder Twins' deaths, all the men in Atlantic City "signed on the dotted line" to stop the killings.

There was no press at the Atlantic City conference. The public learned of it when Capone told the police about it himself after being arrested—quite possibly on purpose—in Philadelphia shortly after the conference. He was arrested by a Philadelphia detective he had known in Florida on charges of carrying a concealed weapon. He made no effort to resist and pleaded guilty at once, earning himself a year in Pennsylvania's prisons. Practically everyone, including the mayor of Philadelphia, felt that Capone had gotten himself jailed deliberately in order to be better protected from gangsters eager to kill him in revenge for the massacre. Even with a peace pact signed, he couldn't have believed he was safe. A year out of the public eye would give things time to cool down.

While in police custody he cheerfully told the whole story of the peace pact in Atlantic City, apparently thinking he wouldn't soon have a chance to tell "the boys" back in Chicago about it in person. Getting the story to the press was the best way to send the news.

Remarkably, Capone spoke candidly about anything the police asked him about, including the notorious murder of William McSwiggin. "Yeah," said Al. "Little Mac was a fine fellow. He was a great friend of mine, always trying to help everybody. I was talking to him in my hotel just before he was shot."

As usual he went right into his routine of presenting himself as a benefactor. "I've been trying to get out of the racket for two years," he said, "but I couldn't do it. Once in, you're always in. The parasites trail you begging for favors and dough. You fear death and worse than death; you fear the parasites of the game, the rats who would run to the police if you didn't constantly satisfy them with money. I'm tired of gang murders and gang shootings. I'm willing to live and let live. I have a wife and an eleven-year-old kid, a boy, whom I idolize, and a beautiful home on Palm Island in Florida. If I could go there and forget it all, I would be the happiest man in the world."

Capone was also asked about the brutal killings the week before, which no one at the time had ascribed to him.

"I'm like any other man," he said. "Three of my friends were killed in Chicago last week. That certainly doesn't get you peace of mind. I haven't had peace of mind in years. Every minute I was in danger of death. Even on a peace errand you're taking a chance at the light going suddenly out."

Minutes later, Capone and Frankie Rio, his bodyguard, were sentenced to a year in prison on the concealed weapons charge. The sentence came only sixteen hours after the arrest.

Capone spent a nightlong stint in Moyamensing Prison—the same prison where Chicago's notorious

Al Capone's mug shot and card from Eastern State, the Philadelphia prison where he did time EASTERN STATE PENITENTIARY

killer H. H. Holmes had been held and hanged a generation before—before being transferred to Holmesburg County Jail, where he was given a prison haircut, outfitted in blue denim, and assigned a number. He gave a massive diamond ring to his lawyer with instructions to get it to Ralph in Chicago.

He was soon transferred to Eastern State Penitentiary, a much cushier jail than the overcrowded pit that was Holmesburg. There Capone set himself up in a very nice cell with rugs and furniture and was allowed to receive visitors such as Ralph Capone and Frank Nitti in the privacy of the warden's office. He gave frequent press conferences, waxing philosophical about what Napoleon could have done in Chicago, among other topics. Given how well Capone was treated, Jonathan Eig, author of *Get Capone,* mused that the warden, "Hard Boiled" Smith, must have gotten his nickname from the way he liked his eggs.

Some have suggested Capone's plan to go to jail as evidence that syphilis was beginning to ravage his brain, but in any case he survived the next several months. He was still in good shape when he was released early nine months later.

As for Joseph Aiello, he was machine-gunned to death in October 1930, punctured by thirty-five steel-coated bullets on the corner of Washington and Cicero. Police were sure it was the work of the Capone gang.

But, as usual, no one was ever convicted.

CHAPTER FOURTEEN

Closing In

While Capone sat in jail, the authorities were closing in, building a case to bring against him upon his release.

In the months after the St. Valentine's Day Massacre in 1929, newly sworn-in President Herbert Hoover sat down with several civic leaders from Chicago to discuss the problem of gangland violence. The men pleaded with the new president, who was then one of the most respected men in the world because of his efforts to keep Europe from starving after World War I. They needed federal help, they told him. Local authorities were powerless against the gangs.

"They gave me chapter and verse," Hoover later recalled, "for their statement that Chicago was in the hands of the gangsters, that the police and magistrates were completely under their control, that the governor of the state was futile, that the federal government was the only force by which the city's ability to govern itself could be restored."

Hoover wasn't entirely convinced that he should get involved; most of the crimes the civic leaders were

One of Al Capone's best-known stunts in his ongoing PR campaign was opening a soup kitchen in 1931. NATIONAL ARCHIVES

talking about were local ones, not something he believed the federal government had any business dealing with. But Capone's growing fame was a thorn in the side of government in general, and his flouting of a federal law was making him a folk hero. Catching so tasty a fly would send a strong message to the countless Capone wannabes out there, not to mention the children who were growing up admiring a criminal.

Hence the order to "get Capone" was given to every agency that could help. The civic leaders who met with Hoover agreed to pay many of the expenses, even funding the nation's first scientific crime lab in order to do ballistics tests on bullets and guns thought to have been used in the St. Valentine's Day Massacre, preparing to make a stronger case against Capone when he finished his short term in Philadelphia.

Hoover himself doesn't seem to have been a great fan of Prohibition. When asked about it, he gave no plans to formally repeal it, but he didn't exactly give it a ringing endorsement either. He described it as "a great social and economic experiment, noble in motive and far-reaching in purpose." The same could be said of communism.

But Hoover's days as a respected president would be short-lived. In October 1929 the stock market crashed and the Great Depression began, and Hoover began a long slide from being one of the world's most respected men to one of its most reviled. By the end of Hoover's term, it would be fair to say that Capone was far more popular than the president.

When Capone heard of the stock market crash in his cell, he joked to his lawyers that "I deny absolutely that I am responsible."

Some months later he was released from jail and journeyed toward Chicago, where he intended just a quick stop to visit relatives before heading back to Miami. But as he journeyed toward the city, it was announced that Chicago police were waiting for him. Not for any particular rap—those charges were still being prepared. But the fact that Pennsylvania had managed to put him in jail hours after his arrival there was horribly embarrassing to the Chicago police, who had never managed to lock him up, and they were determined to save face.

Capone surrendered for questioning after a few days of hiding out, and the chief of police told him he had better get out of town; no one wanted him in Chicago.

An irate Capone had by then already set up a new office in a suite at the Lexington Hotel on Michigan Avenue, a more opulent place than the Metropole had been. After being told to get out of town, he sat at his large mahogany desk, with pictures of George Washington and Big Bill Thompson, a uniquely odd pairing, on the wall behind him as he spoke to Genevieve Forbes Herrick, long one of the best crime reporters in Chicago. His only crime, he told her, was "selling beer and whiskey to the best people. . . . some of our best judges use the stuff."

Capone continued to give great copy. "They talk about me not being on the legitimate," he said. "Why, lady, nobody's on the legit. You know that, and so do they. Your brother or your father gets in a jam—what do you do? Do you sit back and let him go over the road without trying to help him? You'd be a yellow dog if you did. Nobody's really on the legit, when it comes down to cases. You know that."

The limelight had taken a toll on Capone and his family. He brought in his wife and sister, then sent them away after pointing out the streak of gray in his wife's hair to Herrick. "She's only twenty-eight, and she's got gray hair just worrying over things here in Chicago."

Capone himself was only thirty-one years old at this time, though he looked far older, despite the fact that his own hair was not yet gray. He had recently heard that he was not likely to be welcome back in Miami either.

"There's been a change of administration since I was there last," he said. "The brother of one of the officials owns a paper there that's losing a thousand dollars a day. Naturally they got to make news, naturally. So that's why there's all this ballyhoo about me. They got to sell papers."

Indeed, back in Miami Capone filed a writ preventing police from arresting him, but wheels were put in motion to make life for him there as difficult as possible. Though the writ protected him off and on, the *Tribune* joked that he was being arrested in Miami "every few minutes." Capone would have said the same. Authorities would pick him up "for investigation" or "vagrancy" as often as they could, only to let him go later. Miami police were acting on what had become known as "the Chicago Plan": simply arresting Capone whenever they saw him on whatever charges they could think up. For his part, Capone swore out warrants charging the officials with conspiracy, but a judge quickly dismissed them.

Clearly, in the time he'd been in jail, the world had changed. Capone was no longer the beloved figure he had been. People were getting fed up with the exploits they'd once found entertaining. And the gang killings continued. As Capone battled with the Miami authorities, Chicago gangster Red McLaughlin's body was churned to the surface of a drainage canal by a tugboat; it had been thrown into the water wrapped in seventy-five pounds of iron. McLaughlin had been involved in wars over control of taxicab companies; who bumped him off remains a mystery, but you can bet that the name "Capone" was on every lip.

Meanwhile authorities successfully convicted Ralph Capone of tax fraud, a rap that could have earned him as much as twenty-two years in jail, and similar charges were being built against Capone himself.

Even the treasury department knew that most of the stories about Capone were bunk. In a 1931 letter to the "IRS Agent in Charge," a man from the intelligence unit wrote that "Al Capone has been mentioned in connection with practically every major crime committed in Chicago within the last few years; possibly some of the stories are true, but, no doubt, a great deal of the stuff printed originated in the fertile brow of some newspaper reporter or magazine writer."

All through the summer of 1930, Miami authorities worked their best to harass Capone, eventually bringing him to trial on perjury charges, which kept him occupied for much of July. By the end of 1930, he was fed up and reported to be planning to sell his home.

By late 1930 the Capone organization was presumed to be pulling in massive amounts of money, yet Capone had not paid income tax in years.

Something was clearly amiss, but Capone was good at covering his tracks. He held no bank account and was only ever found to have endorsed one check.

He was back in Chicago for the political primaries in early February 1931, where the *Tribune* opened their story about his being back in town by calling him Public Enemy Number 1 and alleging he had contributed $150,000 to Big Bill Thompson's reelection campaign. Capone's contributions wouldn't be enough to keep Thompson in office now. The city had become thoroughly embarrassed by Thompson's antics, and voters instead chose Anton Cermak, despite Thompson's jokes about Cermak's foreign-sounding name (which didn't play as well with the German, Irish, and Polish constituents as his anti-British slanders had). This was, in a way, another signal that Capone's influence was waning. He exercised his usual PR skills, responding to the nation's crippling depression by opening a soup kitchen that offered free soup, sandwiches, and doughnuts to unemployed men; but no amount of PR was likely to save him now.

At the end of February 1931, he was sentenced to six months in jail for contempt of court for feigning illness to avoid a grand jury summons in 1929. His lawyers had said he was "dangerously ill" and couldn't leave Florida, but it was well known that he was attending races and boxing matches at the time. He was set free pending appeal, but things were about to get worse for him: Special Prohibition agents were trailing the gang, engaging their beer trucks in chases. On April 11 a brewery at 3161 South Wabash was raided and fifty thousand gallons of beer were destroyed.

The treasury department had put a young man named Eliot Ness, a twenty-eight-year-old University of Chicago graduate, in charge of catching Capone and his men in their violations of the Volstead Act. He was first mentioned in the *Chicago Tribune* in May 1931, when he and his men caught a beer truck in an alley between Wells and LaSalle after a daring chase from 22nd Street to the Loop. The truck bore the logo of the fictitious "Seamless Tube Company" and contained eleven barrels of beer. Not exactly a huge score, and it was small potatoes compared to the raids that were taking place, and the evidence that was being gathered, outside the limelight. Shortly thereafter, the old Sieben Brewery, site of so much trouble for Torrio, was raided, yielding five truckloads and 4,500 gallons of booze.

A month after this reprise of the Sieben raid, Capone was finally indicted. In addition to chasing beer trucks through the Loop, Ness had been risking his life gathering data about the Capone organization, and now had all he needed. Ness had gathered a very small, elite group of officers who couldn't be bribed. They would come to be known as "the Untouchables," and they had worked diligently to gather evidence against Capone.

When the indictment came down, US Attorney Johnson praised Ness's work, noting that he'd gathered evidence sealing the government's conspiracy case against

Capone at great risk and noting that he and his Untouchables had turned down bribes amounting to many times
their $2,800 annual salaries. Sometimes they'd been
offered $2,000 simply to move down the street when
they were watching for beer trucks.

Despite a general lack of publicity that kept Ness
under the public's radar during the investigation, the
gangsters had known all about him. He received death
threats regularly, and beer trucks ran his car off the
road often. The Capone gang even hired an investigator
of their own to shadow him, attempting to prove that he
wasn't really as squeaky-clean as he was made out to be.

But all his work, digging through whatever records
he could confiscate and tapping phone calls made to
"Snorky," the gang's code name for Capone, paid off. On
June 12, 1931, Capone and sixty-eight of his men were
indicted as conspirators in a $20 million per year beer
conspiracy. The indictment included five thousand separate offenses, most of which consisted of transporting
beer trucks delivering more that $50,000 in beer per day
over a ten-year period.

It was damning evidence, and Capone's men clearly
thought he was finished. Still tapping the wires, Ness and
his men announced that the gang was in heated discus-
sions as to who would take Al's place as head of the outfit.

Days after the indictment, Capone appeared in court
and pleaded guilty. In court he looked haggard and
tired—far, far older than his thirty-two years. There was
no question that he would be serving jail time; it was
only a matter of how *much*. By pleading guilty, Capone
seems to have hoped he could get short sentences for
conspiracy and tax evasion, to be served concurrently.
This would give him a short enough term that he'd still
be a young man when he got out of prison, after which he
could finally settle down.

The trial dragged on throughout the summer as the feds laid bare the extent of the organization's crimes, and the extent to which Capone had evaded the tax collectors. Even John Torrio, Capone's old boss, was brought in as a possible witness, marking his first visit to Chicago in six years. "I am sorry to be back," he told reporters. He wore dark sunglasses, covered his face with a newspaper, and kept a very low profile, spending most of his time sitting on the bench at the courthouse, waiting to see if he would be called.

Capone remained free throughout the summer as the trial dragged on. In September he was even photographed at Wrigley Field, chatting with Gabby Harnett from his front row seat as he and his son, accompanied by Machine Gun Jack McGurn, watched the Cubs beat the White Sox in a charity match. Perhaps the news that Capone was surely going away softened the public on him; stories are told that he was cheered by the crowd when he took his seat.

Capone may have even begun to see a ray of hope; on September 8 his guilty plea was withdrawn. But the case around him remained solid.

Of particular note in the tax evasion trial was the ledger seized at the Hawthorne Hotel in 1926 after the killing of William McSwiggin. The ledger had gathered dust for years before one of the investigators dug it up, but it provided clear evidence that Capone was earning an income from operating the gambling establishment.

Witness after witness came forward to provide evidence that Capone had been spending money. Witnesses attested to his lavish lifestyle, to the amount of money he carried in his pockets. On October 12 alone, eighteen witnesses were rushed through the box to testify as to Capone's life of luxury. Soon the prosecution had detailed everything about Capone's life, right down to what style

IN THE DISTRICT COURT OF THE UNITED STATES

FOR THE NORTHERN DISTRICT OF ILLINOIS

EASTERN DIVISION.

UNITED STATES	)
VS	) NOS. 22852)
	23232) Consolidated.
ALPHONSE CAPONE	)

We, the Jury find the Defendant NOT

GUILTY as charged in Indictment No. 22852 and we find the

Defendant GUILTY on Counts *one-five-nine-thirteen-eighteen*

and NOT GUILTY on Counts *2-3-4-6-7-8-10-11-12-14-15-16-17-19-20-21-22*

Indictment No. 23232.

[jurors' signatures]

Guilty verdict for Capone signed by all the jurors NATIONAL ARCHIVES

of underwear he bought, which was detailed by several clerks from Marshall Field.

Capone seemed bored throughout these revelations, and his attorneys thought the parade of witnesses was a waste of time. When the prosecutor showed the jurors a $275 diamond belt buckle Capone had purchased—one of thirty—Attorney Albert Fink said, "I don't even care enough to object."

The prosecution detailed the three homes Capone maintained—the one on Prairie Avenue, the estate in Miami, and the suite in the Lexington Hotel. Capone had personally bought the furnishings for each of these places. The night clerk at the Lexington testified that the Capone gang had taken up ten rooms; registries showed that Capone had registered as "George Philips" and that he'd received money under the name "A. Costa." The clerk, though, said he had written in most of the names himself—no one would sign the registry, so he'd just made up names on his own.

Several salesmen from Marshall Field testified that Capone had bought shirts ranging in price from $18 to $30 (a price that made the jurors, many of whom came from country towns, gasp). His suits cost $135 each and were bought in half-dozen lots. In later years nearly every clothing store in Chicago would be spoken of as a place frequented by Capone, but the trial made it clear that he did most of his shopping at Marshall Field, just like any other well-to-do Chicagoan of the day. Even Capone had to grin sheepishly as a salesman, one of three from the underwear department who testified, explained that Capone's custom-made "hand glove silk" underwear was made from the same materials used to make ladies' gloves.

The next day the prosecution closed its case without having put Torrio or any other famous gangster on the stand to testify, which seemed rather anticlimactic to reporters. They had hoped for a trial describing all the details of Capone's exciting life; instead they got testimony about his underpants.

The defense didn't have much of a case to make of its own and simply tried to prove that Capone had lost most of his money on horse races. Eight witnesses—a rogue's gallery of Chicago's most notorious bookies—swore that Capone had lost around $200,000 from 1924 to 1929, which may or may not have been deductible from his income in the first place.

The jury deliberated for eight hours and found Capone not guilty on eighteen counts of tax evasion from 1924, 1928, and 1929. But they found him guilty on five others. One lone juror was said to be holding out against a guilty verdict before finally being swayed around 9:30 at night, at which point applause was heard from inside the jury chambers.

Capone had been holed up in his suite at the Lexington, but he put on his coat and hat and took a limousine to the courthouse at around 11 p.m. when he heard a verdict had been reached.

"How are you feeling, Al?" asked a reporter.

Capone gave him a friendly smile. "I'm feeling fine," he said.

"Do you have any comment?"

"Not a thing now," he said. In his seat at the courtroom fifteen minutes after he was informed that the jury had reached a verdict, Capone sat mopping his forehead with one of his silk handkerchiefs and trying his best to smile.

He was informed that he had been found guilty on five counts and was facing seventeen years in prison. He reacted calmly and was joking in the corridor with his friends seconds later, telling reporters "I'm feeling fine" once again, though they could tell he was worried.

The Lexington Hotel was briefly Capone's headquarters. A famous 1980s investigation found his vault there to be empty. PUBLIC RECORD

A week later he was sentenced to eleven years in federal prison and held without bail in the county jail while his lawyers tried to appeal. He continued to make news while he was in jail, and the papers reported that he was a good prisoner. On Thanksgiving he avoided the usual prison fare and dined instead on food sent to him by his mother—a large turkey with all the trimmings, plus a large serving of spaghetti cooked to his personal taste. He divided it among four prisoners (one of whom, papers took care to note, was black) and bought cake and ice cream for every prisoner in the place.

In March 1932 the world was rocked by the kidnapping of famed aviator Charles Lindbergh's infant son. In the midst of the massive manhunt that followed, Capone offered to use his vast underworld connections to find the kidnapper if only he could be let out of prison. This struck people as suspicious at best; one senator even publicly mused that perhaps the Capone gang had kidnapped the baby themselves in order to secure Capone's release (an idea that didn't seem far fetched at all). Various other underworld types made similar offers, but John Torrio, who was by then being investigated for tax fraud of his own, told investigators he couldn't have possibly found the baby and that he thought the kidnapper was probably someone with a personal grudge against Lindbergh, not someone connected to the underworld. (This would turn out to be correct, though the exact details of the case are, as these things almost always are, still a matter of dispute.) In any case, though Lindbergh was said to be willing to accept Capone's help, his release was never secured; the baby was found dead two months later.

Capone's appeal was eventually denied, and after nearly six months in the county jail, a judge ordered his federal prison term to begin. He was put on a train, handcuffed to an auto thief, and sent to Atlanta. As he was taken from jail, a crowd outside wished him well, shouting "You got a bum break, Al." His friends gathered to see him off, and Capone managed a joke about the crowd: "You'd think Mussolini was passin' through."

Eliot Ness personally accompanied Capone from the jail to the train station, determined not only to make sure Capone didn't escape but also that no assassin's bullet was going to stop Capone from serving the time he'd earned. The rest of the Untouchables were present as well.

As Capone boarded the first in a series of trains, he sat in the car's drawing room and smoked cigars while he chatted with guards, seeming like his amiable old self while he posed for the press en route to the Englewood station.

"What do I think I about it?" he asked. "Well, I'm on my way to do eleven years. I've got to do it, that's all. I'm not sore at anybody, but I hope Chicago will be better and the public clamor will be satisfied." He noted, like many others, that Prohibition would probably not last much longer. "Personally," he said, "I'd rather be in a legitimate racket. It don't cost so much. There's too much overhead in my business, paying off [bribes] all the time and replacing trucks and breweries. They ought to make it legitimate, and if they don't they'll find that sending me away won't help Chicago much."

He was in somewhat better shape now than he'd been at his trial; he'd made use of the rowing machines in the county jail and lost ten pounds, leaving him at a still-bulky 255.

From Englewood he rode the train to Coaler, and then to Danville, Illinois. A few hapless hoboes who tried to ride along had to be turned away, despite their pleas that they were just hopping a train, not trying to liberate Capone.

From Danville Capone was sped to Atlanta to begin paying his debt to society, closing the book on the period of Chicago history that would forever be known as "the Capone Era."

Epilogues and Aftermaths

Capone didn't last that long in Atlanta. After finding that he was able to bribe his way into comfort and privilege, authorities had him transferred to notorious Alcatraz Island, the toughest prison in the country. There no one cared who he was; he was even stabbed in the back in 1936. Legend holds that the stabbing came about when Capone tried to cut in line for the barber, saying "Don't you know who I am?" Another convict grabbed the scissors, held them to Capone and said, "If you don't get to the back of the line, I'm gonna know who you *were.*"

Another convict ran ten feet toward Capone from the barbershop as Capone was at work, going between the clothing room and the shower room. He stabbed him in the back, and Capone spun around and returned with a blow of his own. Lucas, the other convict, ended up in solitary confinement; prison officials said Capone had been refusing to give Lucas financial assistance and that Lucas believed Capone had "informed against him."

True or not, Capone was not the powerful man he had been before. Reports of attacks on him in prison were common—one story circulated that prisoners had threatened

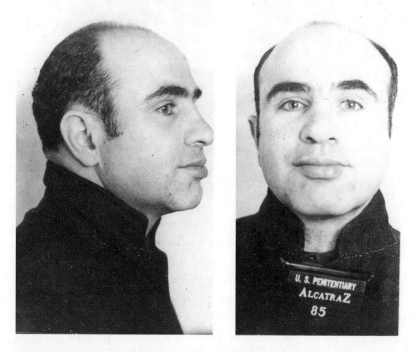

Al Capone's mug shot from Alcatraz, where he was a shell of his former self FBI ARCHIVES

to lynch Capone after suspecting him of "squealing" on an uprising planned by Lucas. According to another report, he was narrowly saved by train robber Roy Gardner from being killed by a window weight thrown by another convict. Only days before the stabbing, it was reported that Capone was under special guard, having been threatened by a group of prisoners after he refused to join them in a plot to blow up the prison.

He may have lost most of the lifestyle he was accustomed to, but the constant threat of death still seemed to follow him around. The combination of the stress of prison life and the slow-burning effects of syphilis on his brain reduced the once-mighty leader to a shell of his former self.

The gang too was in tatters by the time of Capone's release. The repeal of Prohibition cost them a large source of income, and the gang's leaders and top men gradually began to fall away throughout the 1930s and 1940s. Of the major players, only Torrio and Moran survived. Torrio lived in New York as an "elder statesman" of the world of organized crime, seldom getting involved beyond giving advice and dealing with tax charges, until 1957, when he died of a heart attack in a barber's chair in Brooklyn.

Moran died the same year, but under slightly less-dignified circumstances. With his gang effectively wiped out in 1929, and the end of Prohibition depriving him of the easiest source of income, he became known as a drunken has-been. In 1946 he was arrested for robbing a bank messenger in Ohio and sent to prison. Shortly after his release he was arrested for another bank robbery and served a year out of his ten-year term before dying of lung cancer in prison. Practically ruined financially, he was given a pauper's funeral on the prison grounds— far, far away from the graves of his friends and rivals from the old days.

Frank Nitti

When Capone was taken away, Frank "The Enforcer" Nitti became de facto head of the gang. He was a tough enforcer, but apparently not as good at evading police as his old boss had been.

In December 1932 the organization had its headquarters in Room 554 of the LaSalle–Wacker building. While Nitti and six lieutenants were meeting there, four

Frank Nitti, the man known as Capone's "Enforcer" PUBLIC RECORD

detectives led by Detective Harry Lang of Mayor Cermak's office busted in with orders for all present to put their hands in the air. Everyone except Nitti did put his hands up; Nitti busied his hands by shoving a piece of paper into his mouth and chewing it up. Police jumped on him, intent on fishing the paper out of his mouth.

According to the police's story, Nitti drew a pistol and fired at Lang, hitting him. Lang fired his own gun five times, hitting Nitti in the neck, the back, and the chest, nearly severing his spinal chord. He survived, but only barely.

A few months later Mayor Cermak was fatally shot while riding in an open-air car through Miami with president-elect Franklin D. Roosevelt. It was generally said at the time that the assassin's bullet had been meant for Roosevelt, but people have whispered for years that Cermak *was* the intended target, and that the hit had been arranged in revenge for the assault in the LaSalle–Wacker building. One would have to assume, though, that if they'd wanted to kill Cermak, they would have done it elsewhere, some place where they didn't have presidential security to deal with.

Roosevelt, for his part, rode in Capone's old bullet-proof car to his own inauguration.

Throughout the 1930s, after Roosevelt ended Prohibition and forced the gangsters to look beyond bootlegging, Nitti tried to branch the outfit into other directions. In 1943 he and several others were indicted for trying to extort money from the film industry.

Nitti was claustrophobic, and he couldn't stand the idea of being confined in prison. In addition, he was rumored to have been battling terminal cancer. The day before his scheduled grand jury appearance, he took a walk carrying a bottle of now-legal booze and a 32-caliber firearm. As two railroad workers looked on from a distance, he sat against a railyard fence and shot himself in the head. His body was interred in Mount Carmel Cemetery.

Machine Gun Jack McGurn

A hit man can't simply look in the classified ads for work. With Capone gone and with his boxing days long behind him, McGurn was reduced to doing whatever cheap jobs he could throughout the 1930s.

By 1936 he was broke. The other remaining gangsters considered him a has-been and a nuisance. Whether he had truly been the mastermind of the St. Valentine's Day Massacre was never quite known, but local gangsters certainly seemed to think he was, making his presence in the gang a continuing danger in addition to his annoying habit of begging for work or money. Who knew when someone might come bursting in on him for revenge, not caring who else got caught in the crossfire?

By February 1936 he was noted to be jumpy and seemed to expect that the end of his life was coming soon. One friend said he "went pretty near crazy when a tire blew out close to him."

Police said they had fielded panicked calls from McGurn and come to his house to find him locked in his own closet, refusing to come out until he was sure the people who answered the call were, in fact, the police, not assassins. His car, they noted, had recently been repossessed.

On February 15, 1936, a day after the seventh anniversary of the massacre, a couple of friends offered to take him bowling. They went into a bowling alley on Milwaukee Avenue and sat around for several minutes waiting for a lane to become available. As they waited, a few men—one of whom is sometimes assumed to have been Bugs Moran himself—walked in and fired between ten and fifteen shots at McGurn, leaving him dead on the bowling alley floor.

At his feet they left a store-bought valentine showing a grim shadow of a man in front of a house with a FOR SALE sign above the text of a gruesome, badly off-meter poem:

> *You've lost your job, you've lost your dough;*
> *Your jewels and cars and handsome houses!*
> *But things could still be worse, you know . . .*
> *at least you haven't lost your trousers!*

Police at the time said that, from what they knew, it was McGurn who had told Capone of the plot of Scalise and Anselmi to kill him, that it was McGurn who had taken care of the two men in 1929, and that this had secured his place as Capone's right-hand man. This goes against later theories that Frankie Rio,

Capone's bodyguard, was the one who found out about the plot, as well as the stories that Capone had killed the two men personally with a baseball bat. But even if it were true, by May 1929 being Capone's right-hand man wouldn't have been what it once was, and by 1936 McGurn was nothing but an obsolete thug. The killing is still a mystery. Some say it was Moran who killed him in an act of revenge; others say it was Frank Nitti, acting head of the gang, getting the has-been out of the way. Perhaps it was even an unlikely collaboration between the two men.

Officials at Alcatraz said they planned not to tell Capone about the hit, though they assumed he'd soon hear about it through the reliable prison grapevine. McGurn, too, was interred at Mount Carmel.

Frank McErlane

Capone's certainly wasn't the only gang that fell on hard times in the 1930s.

Though the ax murder of a witness saved Frank McErlane, gunman for the old Saltis-McErlane gang, from a long stay in prison, he was in and out of jail for much of the Prohibition era. He was also in and out of sanity.

Long years as a killer began to tear apart the tough man's psyche. In 1931 police found him standing at the corner of 78th and Crandon, spraying the empty street with machine-gun fire. He was shooting, he believed, at the ghosts of the men he had killed.

"They were trying to get me," he gasped. "But I drove 'em off."

As he sat in prison that night muttering to himself, his sister came to the police and told them that the night before, Frank had broken into her house, knocked her to the ground, and bitten her cheek. He was sent off for psychological testing but, remarkably, was back on the street weeks later.

The next month he got into a fight with Marion Miller, his common-law wife, while driving through the city with her. They were both drunk at the time. Miller allegedly pulled a gun and shot at Frank but missed (even though she would have been shooting at point blank range). Frank responded by shooting her to death and then turning around and shooting her two dogs, which were riding in the backseat.

Frank was arrested, and the police found enough guns and ammo to outfit a small militia group in his apartment, but he was eventually released for a lack of evidence. How could they prove McErlane was the shooter when he had so many enemies who might have shot at him and accidentally hit Miller? And even if he *had* been the shooter, how could they say it wasn't self-defense if the stories about Miller shooting first were true?

His gang decided that enough was enough. Rather than killing McErlane, though, they raised a "pension fund" for him and sent him to live on a houseboat on the Illinois River, far away from Chicago in Beardstown, Illinois. It was a fine houseboat—neighbors said it was full of radios, Oriental rugs, and valuable artwork.

The next October, in 1932, he was taken to the Beardstown hospital to battle a case of pneumonia that eventually proved fatal. This made him one of the few gangsters who died of natural causes, but by this time he was living in exile and largely divorced from his own sanity. Hospital officials said his death had, in fact, been something of a violent one. While in the hospital he had lapsed into delirium and had to be held down by four interns while he writhed and shouted out that he was being pursued by some sort of "secret enemy." At one point he jumped out of bed and knocked a nurse unconscious; four loaded pistols were found under his pillow.

When news of his death came, a former friend of his made a statement to reporters. "I don't remember that he ever did anything good in his life. I don't believe he had a friend left."

Sam Genna

One July day in 1935, a man was passing by South Ashland when he saw something: An image that looked vaguely like a woman and her baby had appeared, formed from strands of light, on a blank brick wall. Believing it to be an image of the Virgin Mary and baby Jesus, he fell to the ground. Another came to him, thinking he'd fainted, and then also fell to the ground in devotion.

A crowd began to gather, and the image remained long after the sun had gone down. By the next day a crowd estimated to be in the tens of thousands—perhaps as many as fifty thousand—had gathered in front of the house to see the "miracle," creating havoc for the neighbors. Four hundred police officers were brought in to control the crowd, not unlike the 2005 incident in which a salt stain said to resemble the Virgin Mary appeared on the Fullerton Avenue underpass and drew massive crowds.

Newspapermen began scraping at the image with penknives, believing that it had simply been formed from phosphorescent paint, but to no avail—the image remained. Then, as a man in a house across the street lowered the blinds on his windows, the image vanished and the mystery was solved: The image had been the result of street light bouncing off the window across the street to the wall, with the lace curtain distorting the light and giving it its humanlike appearance.

Immediately reporters ran to the place across the street, the source of the light, and found that it was the home of Sam Genna, one of the few surviving Genna brothers. He was not amused.

"Miracle?" he said. "I don't know nothing. Get out."

Police demanded entrance to the home and pushed their way in, despite Genna's protests that he had visitors (not to mention the fact that they didn't have a warrant). By raising the curtain in the bedroom up and down, they were able to make the "apparition" appear and disappear on the brick wall.

The crowd melted away, leaving Genna in peace. He lived in Chicago for the rest of his life, dying of a heart attack in his home twenty years later.

Al Capone

Various nieces and nephews of Al Capone now have stories about meeting him in Wisconsin, or even in the house on Prairie Avenue, throughout the 1940s. But so far as is known, he lived out most of his last years as something of a recluse at his estate on Palm Island, Florida, after his release from prison. He ventured out to a restaurant now and then, and to church for the wedding of his son, but mostly stayed in his mansion, closely monitored by the FBI, who were tapping his phones to make sure he didn't get into any more racketeering. He made no public return to Chicago and was in no shape to grant interviews most of the time. Though a stay in a Baltimore hospital after his release from jail helped slow his mental deterioration somewhat, he spent his last years going in and out of a childlike state. He had good days and bad.

With a new world war to occupy them, the public had mostly forgotten him by the time of his release, and he only became big news again by dying. Before his demise, curiosity seekers occasionally went to the Miami estate seeking a glimpse of him, but people who saw him on his rare outings seldom seemed to recognize him. Many of his fellow Miamians probably weren't even sure if he was still alive or if he'd died in prison years before. His era, for sure, was over, and he had become one of those people whose insistence on remaining alive beyond their years of fame starts to seem impolite.

A year before his death, Jake "Greasy Thumb" Guzik was asked if Capone was still running things for the gang. Without any apparent fear of reprisal, he snorted that "Al is nuttier than a fruit cake."

In 1946 a "source close to Capone" from his estate told reporters that Al was in no mental shape to run things. "If Capone knows anything about present-day mobs or rackets," he said, "I'd be greatly surprised. He wouldn't know what you were talking about." According to this source, Capone spent most of his days in a peaceful sort of stupor; he wasted hours and hours on his estate's tennis court, puttering around with a tennis racket and aimlessly hitting a ball into a net over and over.

The next year he suffered a stroke and died in his estate, surrounded by his family. He was placed in a $2,000 casket, the nicest available at the time, but the papers wryly noted that his funeral and casket didn't approach the splendor of the funerals and caskets of men like O'Banion, who'd at least had the decency not to outlive the era they'd helped define and to die when they were still a big deal. His remains were said to look shrunken and colorless. Flowers, though, were plentiful, including a seven-foot floral cross. It wasn't like the lavish amount of flowers his brother Frank, or many of his rivals, had been given, but there were still plenty of flowers. Anyway, Capone was certainly past caring by then.

The final resting place of Capone at Mount Carmel Cemetery: The grounds have been worn away by countless visitors.
PHOTO BY AUTHOR

Capone's remains were brought to Chicago, accompanied by his brother Ralph, who was sometimes spoken of in the press as an "elder statesman" for the outfit. Al was initially buried at Mount Olivet Cemetery, then quietly

The interior of James Colosimo's tomb: With notable mystery, the slab says "1919"; Colosimo was shot to death in 1920. PHOTO BY AUTHOR

moved to Mount Carmel in order to thwart the vandals and sightseers who flooded Mount Olivet.

This put him in company with a lot of other gangsters—far more than just the ones an observer had said would see to it that there would be "hell to pay" when "them graves open up." At the time, it had just been Dean O'Banion, Mike Merlo, and Mike Genna in the cemetery. Now they were joined by many of the other Gennas too. And by William Davern, the man whose killing may have inspired the St. Valentine's Day Massacre, and "Three Fingered" White, the man sometimes said to have been behind it, despite the fact that he was in prison at the time. And by Vinnie "The Schemer" Drucci, with his military honors. And by "Hop Toad" Guinta, who had died along with the Murder Twins. Tony Lombardo. "Machine Gun" McGurn. John May. Frank Nitti. Frank Rio. Hymie Weiss. Eventually the motley crew at Mount Carmel would even be joined by Sam Giancana, who became the head of the mob years later before his own assassination in 1975.

Today they rest, either below the ground or in their lavish vaults, on equal terms at last, sharing the peace that only the dead can know.

SELECT BIBLIOGRAPHY

I've perused countless books and articles in preparing this volume. Some were better than others. But even the most unreliable sources can still be a window into how gangsters lived—and live—in the popular imagination.

Books

Asbury, Herbert. *Gem of the Prairie*. New York: Knopf, 1940.

Begreen, Laurence. *Capone: The Man and His Era*. New York: Simon and Schuster, 1994.

Capone, Deirdre Marie. *Uncle Al Capone: The Untold Story from Inside His Family*. New York: Recap Publishing Co, 2012.

Eig, Jonathan. *Get Capone!* New York: Simon and Schuster, 2010.

Iorizz, Luciano J. *Al Capone: A Biography*. Westport, CT: Greenwood Press, 2003.

Keefe, Rose. *Guns and Roses: The Untold Story of Dean O'Banion*. Nashville, TN: Cumberland House Publishing, 2003.

Keefe, Rose. *The Man Who Got Away: The Bugs Moran Story*. Nashville, TN: Cumberland House Publishing, 2005.

Kobler, John. *Capone: The Life and World of Al Capone*. Cambridge, MA: Da Capo Press, 1972.

Lindberg, Richard. *Return to the Scene of the Crime*. Nashville, TN: Cumberland House, 1999.

Lombardo, Richard. *The Black Hand: Terror by Letter in Chicago*. Champaign, IL: University of Illinois Press, 2010.

Parr, Amanda Jane. *Machine Gun Jack McGurn*. Leicestershire, England: Troubadour Publishing Ltd., 2005.

Woolridge, Clifton. *Hands Up: In the World of Crime*. Chicago: Thompson and Thompson, 1901.

Newspaper Articles

Research has led me to peruse literally thousands of newspaper articles, particularly from the searchable archives of the *Chicago Tribune*. Here are a few of my favorites:

"Most Dangerous Neighborhood in Chicago," *Chicago Tribune*, March 3, 1901.

"Death by Dagger, Black Hand Acts," *Chicago Tribune*, November 19, 1907.

"Police Seeking the 'Black Hand,'" *Chicago Tribune*, February 2, 1908.

"Baby Squad Reveals Second Appalling List of Cases," *Chicago Examiner*, July 22, 1908.

"Black Hand Clew [*sic*] Foiled by Fear," *Chicago Tribune*, January 8, 1910.

"100 Black Hand Brigands, 100,000 Italians Sneer at Police," *Chicago Tribune*, March 6, 1910.

"2 Tragedies Due to 'Shotgun Man,'" *Chicago Tribune*, April 28, 1910.

"Sleuth Describes Midnight Revels at Medinah Hotel," *Chicago Tribune*, June 20, 1914.

"Sicilians Pay Toll in Lives to Vendetta," *Chicago Tribune*, June 22, 1914.

"Revenge Rules Little Sicily," *Chicago Tribune*, June 24, 1914.

"Officer 666 Names Gunman," *Chicago Tribune*, July 21, 1914.

"Transfer Capt. Ryan; Jim Colosimo Prisoner," *Chicago Tribune*, July 21, 1914.

"Woman Killed by Avengers of 'Silver King,'" *Chicago Tribune*, June 13, 1915.

"Mother's Life Is Grim Toll Collected by Agents of 'Black Hand,'" *Chicago Examiner*, June 13, 1915.

"Chicago and Its City of Mysterious Death," *Chicago Tribune*, October 3, 1915.

"Colosimo Slain," *Chicago Tribune*, May 12, 1920.

"The Inquiring Photographer," *Chicago Tribune*, September 20, 1920.

"Trap 2 in Ward Murders: Jail Cafe Men as Feud Killers. Cabaret Head Taken as Jazz Blares," *Chicago Tribune*, March 15, 1921.

"Caponi Waves Gun after Crash, Faces 3 Charges," *Chicago Tribune*, August 31, 1922.

"Autos Leap Four Foot Bridge in Thief Chase," *Chicago Tribune*, September 1, 1922.

"Seize Gunmen after Bullets Riddle Cicero," *Chicago Tribune*, September 21, 1922.

"Aldermen Vote for Beer and Wine," *Chicago Tribune*, June 14, 1923.

"One Dead in Rum Gangs War," *Chicago Tribune*, September 8, 1923.

"Who's Who in War of Beer Running Bandits," *Chicago Tribune*, September 18, 1923.

"Gangsters Shoot 2 in Crowded Theatre Lobby," *Chicago Tribune*, January 21, 1924.

"Police in Van Hunt O'Bannion [sic], Man of Flowers," *Chicago Tribune*, March 12, 1924.

"Walk on Roses at Caponi's Bier," *Chicago Tribune*, April 5, 1924.

"Gunman Killed by Gunman; Four Deuces Owner Heads Mystery Feud," *Chicago Tribune*, May 9, 1924.

"'Beer and Roses' O'Bannion [sic] Much Irked by Court," *Chicago Tribune*, July 8, 1924.

"Big Hearted Al Cleans Up 500 Grand on Turf," *Chicago Tribune*, November 3, 1924.

"O'Banion Gang Like Pirates of Olden Days: Beer Trucks Their Gold Ships!" *Chicago Tribune*, November 11, 1924.

"In $10,000 Casket Dean Lies in State," *Chicago Tribune*, November 13, 1924.

"Jail for Torrio," *Chicago Tribune*, January 18, 1925.

"Torrio Is Shot, Police Hunt for O'Banion Men," *Chicago Tribune*, January 25, 1925.

"Inside Cause of O'Banion's Death Is Told," *Chicago Tribune*, January 1, 1925.

"Kill Two Cops, City Aroused," *Chicago Tribune*, June 14, 1925.

"320 Seized in Gang Raids," *Chicago Tribune*, June 15, 1925.

"Torrio Fortifies His Jail Cell; Rumors of War," *Chicago Tribune*, June 25, 1925.

"Gennas in Terror, Tony Dies," *Chicago Tribune*, July 9, 1925.

"Samoots Dies in Silence, Fails to Wed," *Chicago Tribune*, November 13, 1925.

"Hunt New Gang for Machine Gun Foray on Caponi," *Chicago Tribune*, September 22, 1926.

"Kill Drucci in Drive on Ballot Thugs," *Chicago Tribune,* April 5, 1927.

"'You Can All Go Thirty' Is Al Capone's Adieu," *Chicago Tribune,* December 6, 1927.

"Al Capone, Reformer," *Milwaukee Journal,* December 25, 1927.

"Kill Lombardo, Mafia Chief," *Chicago Tribune,* September 8, 1928.

"Slay Doctor in Massacre," *Chicago Tribune,* February 15, 1929.

"Trace Killers: Lid on City," *Chicago Tribune,* February 16, 1929.

"Capone Opens Florida Manner to the Gentry," *Chicago Tribune,* February 19, 1929.

"3 Slain: Scalise, Anselmi?" *Chicago Tribune,* May 8, 1929.

"Capone Takes Cover in Jail," *Chicago Tribune,* May 18, 1929.

"Capone's Story: By Himself: 'Just a Beer Man, The Best People Buy It,'" *Chicago Tribune,* March 22, 1930.

"Gangland Years Make Wreck of Frank McErland," *Chicago Tribune,* June 7, 1931.

"Capone's Trail of Gold Traces in Luxury Sales," *Chicago Tribune,* October 13, 1931.

"Capone Treats to Cake, Ice Cream at Jail," *Chicago Tribune,* November 27, 1931.

"Altruism Stirs Tough Eggs in Hunt for Baby," *Chicago Tribune,* March 12, 1932.

"Capone Gang Chief Sinking," *Chicago Tribune,* December 20, 1932.

"Al Capone Dies in Florida Villa," *Chicago Tribune,* January 26, 1947.

Government Documents

Treasury Department Letter to Internal Revenue Agent in Charge, Chicago IL. In re: Alphonse Capone, July 8, 1931.

Treasury Department Letter to Chief Intelligence Unit. In re: Alphonse Capone, December 21, 1933.

Helvering, Guy T., Intelligence Unit. A Narrative Briefly Descriptive of the Period 1919 to 1936.

Assorted death certificates.

ABOUT THE AUTHOR

William Griffith is known to his friends as "Wild Bill" but actually lives a quiet life with his dogs in a small apartment beneath the El tracks on Lake Street—you get used to the noise after a while. His doorknob was salvaged from the rubble of the Lexington Hotel, and the apartment is reputed to have once been the home of a member of the Genna brothers gang. His grandfather was a gangbuster in northern Missouri.